WESKER'S DOMESTIC PLAYS

Arnold Wesker's

DOMESTIC PLAYS

The Friends

Bluey

Men Die Women Survive

Wild Spring

OBERON BOOKS
LONDON

WWW.OBERONBOOKS.COM

This collection first published in 2012 by Oberon Books Ltd

521 Caledonian Road, London N7 9RH

Tel: +44 (0) 20 7607 3637 / Fax: +44 (0) 20 7607 3629

e-mail: info@oberonbooks.com

www.oberonbooks.com

A catalogue record for this book is available from the British Library.

PB ISBN: 978-1-84943-160-6

E ISBN: 978-1-84943-691-5

Cover photograph by Nobby Clark

Contents

THE FRIENDS

'If the root be in confusion, nothing will be well governed'

CONFUCIUS: 'The Great Digest'
Translated by Ezra Pound

'Now let us sleep until the world becomes morning'

ALI MIRDREKVANDI: *About General Burke*
and his men on the milky way

Author's Note

Confronted for the first time with directing the première of my own play, I discovered myself in the position of being able to shape the internal rhythms as I had written them. These rhythms are here indicated by asterisks in the printed text.

For Charlotte

First performed by Stockholm's Stadsteater at the Lilla Teatern, on 24 January 1970, directed by Arnold Wesker, designed by Teresa Gogulska, with the following cast:

ESTHER	Jane Friedmann
MANFRED	Hakan Serner
CRISPIN	Per Myrberg
TESSA	Gurie Nordwall
SIMONE	Gun Arvidsson
MACEY	Olof Bergstrom
ROLAND	Gosta Ekman

First performed in Great Britain at the Roundhouse, on 19 May 1970, directed by Arnold Wesker, designed by Nicolas Georgiadis, with the following cast:

ESTHER	Susan Engel
MANFRED	Ian Holm
CRISPIN	Roy Marsden
TESSA	Anna Cropper
SIMONE	Lynn Farleigh
MACEY	John Bluthal
ROLAND	Victor Henry

Extensively revised and edited forty-two years later for this edition by Arnold Wesker, March 2012

Characters

ESTHER

MANFRED

CRISPIN

TESSA

SIMONE

MACEY

ROLAND

All are between the ages of 40 and 45.

ACT ONE

SCENE ONE

In a large bed, richly covered and coloured maroon, lies ESTHER. Though ill and tired from her illness, yet she is at work slowly cutting with scissors round the shape of an enlarged old (1911) sepia photograph of her mother.

This is to be added to a mosaic of old photographs – some enlarged, some their original size – which she is building up on an old screen to the left of her bed. Each photograph is of a member of her family: aunts, uncles, cousins, grandparents. It is an area of the set rich in brown, black and white tones, and nostalgia.

Helping ESTHER is her lover ROLAND.

MANFRED, her brother, sits reading and writing notes by a large, old carved desk.

CRISPIN, a friend and partner, sits restlessly at the foot of her bed, constructing his own invented toy.

Hanging behind the bed, jarring yet touching, is a portrait of Lenin.

Near the desk is a re-creation of the Crick-Watson model of the D.N.A. molecule of heredity, two-thirds done.

ESTHER: Only children's faces are really beautiful. Little girls with bows and broderie anglaise; spontaneous, cruel, full of uninhibited love, like tigers. The rest is stupid and vulgar, brutal and pompous. You're not listening, Manfred.

MANFRED: I am, Ketzel, I am. Just a few more lines.

ESTHER: Except the sound of French, that's beautiful; and Russian icons and pre-Raphaelites and Venetian chandeliers.

ROLAND: Last night I slept very soundly. Long and deep.

MANFRED: *(Reading.)* 'The electron is a completely universal fundamental particle ...'

ROLAND: I can't remember the last time I slept so soundly.

MANFRED: '...For all practical purposes it is indestructible and is at present in the universe in inexhaustible numbers...'

ESTHER: And Baroque churches and houses, fountains and market-places and wine and the cooking of friends and the sound of friends.

ROLAND: And because of that long sleep everything about me is sharp and alive.

MANFRED: 'Electron devices and electronic techniques can therefore be used as effectively in any terrestrial environment as in the near-vacuum of outer space with unrivalled speed of response and sensitivity and...'

ESTHER: Stop it, Manfred.

MANFRED: '...and can convey information more efficiently than any other kind...'

ESTHER: It's lunacy.

MANFRED: '...and lend themselves to the control and regulation of small or large amounts of power.'

ESTHER: You surround yourself with books which you start and never finish.

ROLAND: I can't explain how beautiful that sleep was.

ESTHER: A book of essays brings you to the study of architecture; the book on architecture brings you to a history of cities.

ROLAND: I can isolate sounds and tastes and smells.

ESTHER: The impact of cities brings you to sociology; sociology leads you to science and electronics; and electronics involves you in trying to understand theories totally incomprehensible to you.

CRISPIN: Look at that model. It grows, without touching it, it grows.

ESTHER: Then he starts on another essay – and he's off again.

CRISPIN: What *is* an essay?

ESTHER: An essay on Marxist theories of art brings him to a study of the history of revolutions, which introduces him to Voltaire, who is insufficient, so he goes on to the Paris Commune which brings him back to Marx again.

CRISPIN: One man's digest of another man's thoughts. That's all an essay is.

ESTHER: And we have to listen each time he makes a leap forward to start another circle, and the room becomes cluttered with books that he buys and he buys and he buys in a great fever. That's what you've got, Manfred, a great fever.

ROLAND: Esther, lovely, don't, you'll tire yourself out.

CRISPIN: *(To MANFRED.)* Come and sit with your sister, you callous bastard.

MANFRED: *(Book in hand.)* Well I ask you, listen to this: '…we are moving into phases of creative disorder; everywhere the lines are blurred. Physics and biology have reached outside their classic bounds; the important work is being done within the shifting, undogmatic contours of 'middle fields' such as biochemistry, molecular biology or physical chemistry…'

CRISPIN: That model, just look at it.

MANFRED: Well, news like that terrifies me.

CRISPIN: And that model terrifies me.

ESTHER: And he grows bald and he has headaches and he refuses to wear glasses.

MANFRED: Well, doesn't it terrify you?

CRISPIN: Everything terrifies me. Babies, dogs, flies, lightening.

ESTHER: And English lawns with cats, and Italian renaissance music and fragile, lily-like, art-nouveau girls. Beautiful!

MANFRED: '…we are moving into phases of creative disorder; everywhere the lines are blurred…' Good God!

ESTHER: Manfred, please. Can't you see I want as much of you as I can get?

MANFRED: All my life you'll have me, Kitten.

ESTHER: Will I, Manfred? In the grave, too?

MANFRED: *(Coming to her.)* I'm a pig. I'm sorry, Ketzel.

> *MANFRED and ROLAND straighten the crumpled sheets; she smiles and enjoys their fussing. They step back and regard her.*

Good God, how exquisite you look, like a doll.

ESTHER: Fragile you mean, and pale – like a sick child. Oh, I get tired so quickly.

MANFRED: That wasn't quickly. You've been talking for the last two hours – a steady drone while I was reading.

CRISPIN: She used to be so silent and shy.

ESTHER: She used to have nothing to say; now she'd give long speeches if she could, in public.

CRISPIN: What would your speeches be, Ketzel?

ESTHER: Long lists of all the things I really care about, and why. Who do I hate, who do I love; what do I value, what do I despise; what pleases, what offends me? And when I knew, I'd nail them to the front door.

MANFRED: Sleep, Ketzel, and by the time you wake you'll smell hot toast and thick coffee.

ESTHER: It's such a funny thing, sleep. A body curls itself up, closes its eyes and waits. It does absolutely nothing else, a few turns perhaps, but just lies, passively, waiting for something to happen to it.

MANFRED: Sleep. *(Kissing her.)* Lovely eyes, lovely lips. No one's leaving, sleep.

> *Pause. Regards the photo montage.*

Our grandfather and grandmother from Odessa. Our mother, aged nineteen. Her brothers, Theo, Nachum, Abraham. Their children, their children's children…the cousins we've never seen…

> *They move away from the bed.*
>
> *CRISPIN hugs himself into a red velvet wing-backed armchair.*
>
> *ROLAND sits on the floor at the foot of the bed in a simple Yoga position.*
>
> *MANFRED returns to his model.*

CRISPIN: *(To ROLAND.)* Well that's cruel, I say that's cruel. She, your sweetheart, so ill, and you – you sit, contemplating, peacefully.

MANFRED: She's not *so* ill, Crispin. The blood-count was better yesterday.

CRISPIN: She's dying, Manfred, face it.

MANFRED: We don't know that.

CRISPIN: Say it to yourself: my sister's dying.

MANFRED: We don't know –

CRISPIN: Say it to me and to Roland.

MANFRED: We don't know for certain.

ROLAND: *(Wanting to end talk of dying.)* That lunch –

* * *

– I tasted each part of it, my throat separated each part, sharply. And those smells and sounds. It's as though I'm hearing the sound of velvet for the first time, and the movement of wood from the joints in the furniture. Listen. Can't you hear the tiniest shifting of everything in the room? *(Beat.)* I think I'm turning into an aesthete.

> *CRISPIN rises suddenly, and moves to draw the curtains across the window.*

MANFRED: But it's still daylight, you're shutting out the light.

CRISPIN: Candles. Light candles.

MANFRED: Candles? Now?

CRISPIN: We have candles, don't we? Well, light them.

ROLAND: Pull those curtains back, Crispin, there's nothing to be frightened of.

CRISPIN: You're also frightened, you. But you won't admit it, will you?

MANFRED: Crispin!

CRISPIN: Well, he is, and you – playing around with your molecules of heredity. Who the hell wants to know how the mess happened anyway?

MANFRED: Crispin, hush.

CRISPIN: Candles! Light candles!

MANFRED: *(Hugging him.)* Crispin, hush.

> *CRISPIN rejects him and returns to his chair alone.*

We'll light them.

> *MANFRED lights four candles in the candelabra. He cannot work, so they all sit in the flickering glow.*

ROLAND: And I'm going to stop eating from now – except foods with primary tastes, like fruit and meat.

CRISPIN: I'm cold.

> *MANFRED goes to the bedside and takes the cover, which he lovingly wraps around CRISPIN.*
>
> *CRISPIN reaches to a record-player.*

And music, let's have music.

MANFRED: Esther!

CRISPIN: Esther won't mind. She likes waking to music.

> *It is the second part of Mahler's eighth symphony.*

MANFRED: What do I hate, who do I love; what do I value, what do I despise; what pleases, what offends me? All those questions. Now.

ROLAND: And I shall cease to be obese. It's so humiliating to have a body that won't do what you want it to do.

CRISPIN: Do you know I've stopped reading in the lavatory. I began feeling it was an insult to the writer.

ROLAND: Funny, it's quite the reverse for me. I'm so disgusted with the act, I need a book to help me rise above it.

> *Pause.*

I sometimes wish we didn't belong to this generation. There were times when to pick our nose and put our feet up on chairs and swear in front of girls and find it thrilling when they swore straight back was all delight. Such defiance, such dignity. But it's a minor kind of dignity I feel, now, such a tiresome sort of defiance. There's no…no nobility in it. No…no majesty.

CRISPIN: Like this room. No majesty here. Dishonest, that's what it is. We own five shops selling twentieth-century interiors which we've designed, *we've* designed, mind you, and yet look at this room. Bits and pieces from other men's decades.

MANFRED: We've neglected those shops.

ROLAND: I hate them. Everything about them. I hate them.

CRISPIN: You know why? We didn't design what we *knew* was good. We asked 'the people'.

ROLAND: So's to give the people a sense of 'participation'!

CRISPIN: In the name of 'democracy'!

ROLAND: Couldn't say our tastes were superior to theirs –

CRISPIN: – that would place us in a class we were asking them to overthrow! *(Beat.)* What long discussions we had.

ROLAND: There is a character in an Eliot novel who asked: 'Don't you think men overrate the necessity for humouring everybody's nonsense, till they get despised by the very fools they humour?'

CRISPIN: What lovely, long discussions we had.

MANFRED: Esther keeps complaining: 'Why are you here all the time? Who's looking after the shops?'

CRISPIN: Tell her. I keep saying we should tell her.

MANFRED: What good would it do, Crispin?

CRISPIN: We're going to be bankrupt. She should know.

MANFRED: She'll know soon enough.

CRISPIN: And why haven't the girls come?

ROLAND: Auditors are long-winded.

CRISPIN: You should have gone with them.

ROLAND: We all should have gone. Poor girls. Not even they care any longer. Only they're women, tenacious, heavy with loyalties – like un-milked cows.

> *Pause.*

I wonder if your eyes change colour when you turn into an aesthete?

CRISPIN: That music. Turn it off. Please!

CRISPIN seems to want to vanish into the armchair.

MANFRED turns off the music at its most vibrantly passionate passage.

Silence.

ROLAND: Music never could soften pain.

CRISPIN: *You* don't think she's suffering pain, do you?

ROLAND: She aches, that's all.

CRISPIN: She says she aches but we all know –

ROLAND: There's fatigue, weariness, but only that.

CRISPIN: You're a fool, Roland, after all her bleeding and that bruising – you don't want to believe it.

ROLAND: When Esther suffers pain so will I, that's how I'll know.

MANFRED: That's wrong, Roland. Esther wouldn't like that. You mustn't make predictions like that to yourself...

CRISPIN: Listen to his voice...

MANFRED: ...not even in a joke. I know you, you make predictions then can't find reasons why you shouldn't fulfil them.

CRISPIN: How softly he speaks, still.

MANFRED: Stop talking about me as if I wasn't here.

CRISPIN: Gentle Manfred. Where does he find all that gentleness?

MANFRED: And stop pretending cruelty, Crispin. No one believes you.

ROLAND: Do you ever think how strange, but really strange people are? There was once a man I knew, shortly after we'd opened the partnership, who asked me to arrange the inside of a large room like a grand concert hall, with pastel murals showing vistas of people arranged on seats and in boxes listening to music. And into this room he invited his friends every Sunday morning to watch him conduct gramophone records.

Pause.

He wasn't an aesthete!

CRISPIN: I remember, once, when I was working on my own, a woman rang me up, at three in the morning. She'd sat up all night looking at her bedroom wall. It had to be red. There and then. It had to be painted red. And I rode to her house five miles away, on a bicycle, hopefully imagining it was a ruse to get me into her bedchamber in a needful hour. But it wasn't. There on the floor, when I arrived, was a brush and a tin of red paint and I had to work, while she watched, for three hours, sitting up in bed. And after it she paid me twenty pounds. One wall.

Pause.

Manfred says nothing. He doesn't find the world strange or evil, only lovely and interesting. Explanations for everybody. Lovely compassions, tender opinions.

MANFRED: Stop talking about me as if I weren't here.

CRISPIN: You still think we love each other, don't you?

MANFRED: And don't shout at me.

CRISPIN: If only he didn't deny the existence of evil. That's what I can't bear.

ROLAND: Stop it, Crispin.

CRISPIN: Evil, evil, Manfred, chant it, lad.

ROLAND: Crispin!

CRISPIN: Evil, Manfred. They took a child from its mother, Manfred, and smashed its head against the wall. Evil!

ROLAND: Stop it or go home.

CRISPIN: A willingness to do a thing which is the opposite of goodness. A *willingness*, a love, an active willingness. Evil! Evil, evil, evil! Say it, Manfred.

ROLAND: Crispin!

CRISPIN: Say it!

Pause.

MANFRED: Our trouble, Crispin, us lot, the once-upon-a-time bright lads from up north, is that we've no scholarship. Bits and pieces of information, a charming earthiness, intelligence and cheek, but – no scholarship. Look at these books here. *(He picks up a pile and throws them round him.)* Renan, Taine, Kirkegaarde, Wittgenstein, Spengler, Plato, Jung, Homer, Vico, Adorno, Lukacs, Heine, Bloch – you've not heard of half of them, have you? And half of them, two-thirds, I'll never read.

Do you know, new knowledge disrupts me. Because there's no solid rock of learning in this undernourished brain of mine, so each fresh discovery of an idea doesn't replace but undermines the last; it's got no scholarly perspective by which to evaluate its truth or its worth.. So when I sometimes get a feeling that two people in love or one man afraid of death might be a supreme consideration, along comes this man with his 'we are moving into phases of creative disorder' and his 'everywhere the lines are blurred' and I've no defence. He sounds so right, I think, and besides – he's got scholarship. Evil? You want me to confess to the knowledge of evil? I confess it. I say it – evil! So? And what shall I do with *that* bit of knowledge?

CRISPIN: Only a bloody Jew would discover evil with sadness instead of despair.

MANFRED: *(Moving to ESTHER's bed.)* I'll never do anything right for you, Crispin.

Look how she sleeps; so sweet. What the hell do I care for the dead knowledge of evil when I'm blessed with a sister as sweet as this?

> *Pause, listening.*

The girls are coming.

> *TESSA and SIMONE, the last two of the FRIENDS, enter with MR MASON, 'MACEY', aged about fifty-five, Jewish, who has been the manager of their main shop.*

TESSA: Yes, the girls *are* coming and what's more they're hot and mad and full of war. Tell them, Macey.

MACEY: Tessa, I told you, no alarms.

SIMONE: *(Hanging up coats.)* Not now, Tessa.

TESSA: And what are we in darkness for? Who's drawn the curtains?

> *She angrily blows out the candles and violently draws aside the curtains.*

TESSA: Are you going mad! Candles?

MACEY: She doesn't listen.

TESSA: Broad daylight and you light candles?

SIMONE: Come, Tessa, take off your shoes. Crispin, fetch a bowl of water.

> *Moves to pour drinks.*

TESSA: They sit fair, square and immovable.

MANFRED: Tessa, lower your voice – Esther.

TESSA: I'll wake her, shall I wake her?

SIMONE: Enough now! Tessa!

TESSA: You'll listen to her, the darling's dying, you'll listen to her.

SIMONE: You've frightened them enough.

* * *

> *TESSA sits in an eighteenth-century chair and takes off her shoes.*

TESSA: Twenty years! Finished! Like that!

SIMONE: Roland, move off your haunches; it's tantalizing.

TESSA: And I've told them and told them, and they don't listen.

SIMONE: Macey, take a seat.

TESSA: *(Moving to stool by coffee table.)* I hate that chair.

> *SIMONE joins her, massages her feet.*

Tell them, Macey.

MACEY: That's not nice, Tessa, to come straight away to a house and not say hello or ask about people. No grace, your generation.

ROLAND: Hallelujah!

SIMONE: *(To CRISPIN.)* Please!

MANFRED: *(Picking up a book.)* Macey, I've a new thought for you.

TESSA: Enough prevaricating. Macey's got something to say.

MANFRED: There's a professor of comparative literature here says that the coming of print gave man a one-dimensional view of the world and crippled all his other perceptions.

TESSA: Let Macey tell you the news.

MANFRED: Ssh! He says 'the phonetic alphabet makes a break between eye and ear' and man has used this to change from 'the tribal to the civilized sphere' and 'since it's obvious that most civilized people are crude and numb in their perceptions' then it follows that the printing press has held back progress for five centuries and we must start all over again to unify the senses.

TESSA: Crispin, you stop them.

MANFRED: Isn't that staggering? I find that one thought alone upsets everything, everything.

TESSA: Manfred, let Macey speak, for Christ's sake.

MACEY: What's so staggering about it? What staggers me more is that print has been around for the last five hundred years and not only is two-thirds of the world still illiterate, but even those who could read never did and still don't, so where's his proof? How can you be crippled by something you never engaged in? Maybe it's the other way round? Maybe they got crippled because they *didn't* read.

MANFRED: But words act like dams, he says.

MACEY: Nonsense! I've never heard such nonsense. Lovely things like words? 'Languor' – listen to it. It sounds like what it is – full of lingering and longing: 'languor!' 'Anguish', 'miasmatic', 'crackling', 'surreptitious', 'sonorous', 'asinine'. Lovely words. Dams? Gates more like, to everywhere, to every-possible-where. Can you think of better?

TESSA: He's like an old grandmother. *(To MACEY.)* You're like an old grandmother.

ROLAND: He *is* an old grandmother.

CRISPIN: Leave him alone, he's *my* grandmother.

MACEY: If you're listening to a man talking and you're not sure you like what he says, what helps you to be sure? He sounds right, but something nags at you. To *feel* he's wrong is not enough, you want to identify it, more precisely.

TESSA: Identify it, then; for Christ's sake identify it!

MACEY: He's attacking the world, let's say. He's critical. That's good, very good to be critical. The world is a stupid, ignorant, vulgar place, he's saying. And you agree; most of the time it is. But still, something's missing, he doesn't sound quite right, if only you can find the right words for it. What will describe, as near precisely as matters, what's wrong about what he's saying?

TESSA: Have you ever heard a man talk so much?

MACEY: Let me talk! How can I know what I'm thinking if I don't talk? The word, you're looking for the word to describe what's wrong with what he's saying. Find the word and you'll understand. He's critical, yes; he's sad, but – but what? 'Dispassionate'! That's it, that's the word. And suddenly all the other words that sounded good – like 'critical' and 'sad' – are pushed just a little aside and a new view of him filters through. *His* sadness has nothing to do with the suffering of the world, it has to do with his image of himself. He wants you to see him being sad. The word 'dispassionate' has enabled you to suspect him of wanting to see the world as full of ignorance because, by comparison, he can then appear clever. And that leads you further; *because* you've discovered he's dispassionate you then recognize that the details of his criticism are barren. There! another word that's come to you – 'barren' and sterile.

MANFRED: There's something wrong.

TESSA: Will you please let Macey tell you.

MANFRED: You sound right but there's something wrong. I'll think about it.

TESSA: Macey?

MACEY: All right, all right. It's a rotten business, it's my right to procrastinate. There! 'procrastinate', wonderful word –

TESSA: Macey!

* * *

29

MACEY: You're bankrupt! Manfred, Roland, Crispin – I think it's what you all wanted and it's happened. You're bankrupt.

CRISPIN: *(Moving to get the bowl of water.)* Good!

TESSA: Good?

CRISPIN: Yes, good!

MACEY: Good?

CRISPIN: Good! Good!

MACEY: But I don't understand you anymore. My lovely boys given up?

MANFRED: We're not boys any more, Macey. You've grown old with us so you haven't noticed.

MACEY: But you've gotten unhealthy, closed, incestuous. Is it a holiday you want? Go away then, all of you. I'll look after things, day and night I'll look after things, like always, I'll stay with it. I'll sell things, I'll mortgage my house, we'll all sell things. Macey'll stay. Wouldn't I do that for you? Wouldn't I do anything for you?

ROLAND: Spell it out, Macey.

MACEY: You're not listening, even.

No response, they wait.

Well, I've cracked each problem as it came up. I've kept my eye on the accounts, daily, there's no mess but there's no money. The sum is simple. You've neglected to order what you once knew would sell, you've not commissioned new designs like you used to, you've not done any yourselves, and so now sales don't equal bills and they've not been equalling bills for a long time, and the reserve capital is eaten up

CRISPIN leaves.

Tessa wanted me to tell you because she said you wouldn't listen to her, so I've told you and so now I'm going – except I want to see my Esther.

ROLAND: Stay, Macey. It's not so bad. We're not really bankrupt. I wish we were, but unfortunately we've all got large private accounts. At least I have. The business will fold because we want it to, but the bills will be paid and adequate notice given to the staff. So now let's forget the shops, let's not talk about it this evening, or ever more.

Pause.

I'm becoming an aesthete.

MACEY: A what?

MANFRED: He's turning into an aesthete.

MACEY: He's turning into an aesthete? It's possible? He's had an operation or something?

ESTHER: *(Wakes up suddenly and irritably.)* Where's my coffee?

TESSA: Esther!

ESTHER: It's never ready when I want it. You neglect me as well?

TESSA: *(Going to her.)* Esther, hello, my kitten. The day's over. We're all home, together again. How are you now? You look so rested. Look at her, Simone, she has colour again.

ESTHER: Never mind my colour, where's my coffee and my hot toast? What are you all doing here? Macey, why are you here? Go back to work. I won't have all this idleness. I've never been able to bear idleness.

MACEY: Esther! Such shouting.

ESTHER: And my coffee – where is it?

MANFRED: Hush, Ketzel. I'll get it for you. You've woken up earlier than usual, that's all.

MACEY: What do you mean 'go back to work'? The day's over. And if it wasn't over, I couldn't come and visit you? What's this?

ESTHER: Look, Macey, bruises. My body, full of bruises, look at me, my arms, my legs, full of pain. I'm racked with pain and you all stand around.

ROLAND: You haven't got pain, Esther.

TESSA: Shut up, Roland.

ROLAND: She hasn't got any pain, she keeps saying she has and you believe her and I know she hasn't got any pain.

> *CRISPIN enters with a bowl, a jug of hot water and a towel.*

CRISPIN: Tessa, your water.

MANFRED: I'll get your coffee and toast, Ketzel. *(Leaves.)*

MACEY: 'Ketzel'. I had a sister we used to call Ketzel: tiny kitten. She became a mathematician, very rabbinical she was. Esther, I got a story for you. A rabbi died and went to heaven and he managed to get a word in edgeways with God and he said, 'Hey, God, is it true you chose the Jews?' and God said, 'Yes,' and the rabbi said, 'Well, do me a favour and choose someone else.' Isn't that funny? Good, she laughs. It's all right then.

ESTHER: *(Despite laughing.)* But I'm still so tired.

> *ROLAND rushes from room.*

TESSA: Lie back, then, Kitten. Here, lift a little and I'll re-arrange your pillows. There, they need punching. Better? Do you want more?

SIMONE: Come on, Tessa, your water's here. It'll get cold.

> *SIMONE kisses ESTHER who closes her eyes and dozes again.*
>
> *Then she urges TESSA back to a chair, places her feet in the hot water and washes them.*

CRISPIN: Come on, Macey, there's nowt left for thee nor me to do except drink.

MACEY: And why the dialect all of a sudden?

CRISPIN: So's not to see the seriousness of it.

MACEY: I didn't intend to stay. Say my little piece and go, thats what I intended.

CRISPIN: Eat with us, Macey. Tha's not done that in a long while; we're not together much longer.

MACEY: I feel uncomfortable, Crispin, and hurt. I love you all still, but you don't take it like you used to. I'm like a father intruding on his children's privacy. It's so large, this house, and full of gloom. Not like the shop – full of light and brightness there, but here – Old Nick lives here.

CRISPIN: Aye, it seems like it right now because we're all living together. Usually, though, it's only Manfred, Esther and Roland. But with Esther's dying –

MACEY: Stop that! Are you mad?

CRISPIN: With Esther being ill – we've all camped down.

MACEY: You don't leave each other alone, you've not been apart for weeks now. Is that what you want?

CRISPIN: We've been brought together, like, an' now noa one of us can bear to lose sight of t'other.

MACEY: It's not good, Crispin. Tell them that. Tell them that it's not good.

CRISPIN: Nay. It's very good, Macey. We should've always lived like it, good! *Wilt* tha stay?

MACEY: I don't know. I'll drink my drink and think about it.

Pause.

TESSA: Crispin, come and brush my hair.

CRISPIN: Not while Simone's washing your feet I won't.

TESSA: All right, Simone, thanks, enough now.

> *SIMONE, hurt, leaves TESSA to soak her feet.*
>
> *CRISPIN brushes TESSA's long hair.*

SIMONE: Another drink, Macey?

MACEY: Please. *And* you'll make the dinner, won't you?

SIMONE: Yes.

MACEY: Silent Simone, working for everyone.

SIMONE: That's my pleasure, Macey. Besides, even when I try to talk they shut me up. My class credentials aren't acceptable, you know!

MACEY: Ha! Class! One day will I give them a lesson about class; such nonsense I've had to take from them all these years.

SIMONE: Such nonsense we've both had to take, eh, Macey?

MACEY: Poor Simone, you do no one thing and you do everything.

SIMONE: It's because I can do no *one* thing that I do everything. I'm very useless, Macey.

> *She reaches to continue work on a small tapestry on stand.*

MACEY: Then do something for me, Simone, sell the business.

SIMONE: Sell it? Me?

MACEY: Don't let them wind it down. Find somebody to buy it. You'll get a good price and I can stay with it. I'm too old for change.

SIMONE: You sell it, Macey. If you want to stay there you sell it.

MACEY: But I'm only a manager, you're a director.

SIMONE: Act on our behalf. I give you permission. We don't care.

MACEY: Extremes! Everything you do is extreme. After one shop was a success you didn't open another *one* but another *five*! Esther never designed small tapestries, they had to be enormous, for cathedrals and boardroom walls and airports. And look at all those books. Manfred doesn't buy one at a time, but whole libraries, from professors who die, desperately hoping their books will hand on their cleverness. And Roland. A brilliant man, brilliant! Figures were games for him. Look at him now. He wants to become an aesthete! Once he wanted to be a voluptuary. From one extreme to another. Excessive. Six of the most talented people in the field and you're all – you're all – well I don't know what you're all doing. I don't understand it. It's not anything I understand at all.

> *Pause.*

SIMONE: The streets are filled with strange, young people, Macey. Beautiful boys and girls with long hair and colourful bit and pieces they buy from our shop. All styles – Victorian, art-nouveau, military – as though they're attracted by the pomp and circumstance of traditions they're supposed to hate. And they want only one thing, these people. To love. It's as though they're surrounded by so much ugliness and greed that they have to spend all their time convincing themselves that beauty exists. And they try to be frightened of nothing.

Anyhow, whatever it is, listen to this – two of them came into the shop today and held out their hands. In one hand was a black handkerchief containing money, in the other hand a packet of plain biscuits. And one of them said, 'Have some money,' like that, 'Have some money,' as though he were offering me a cigarette. And do you know I was embarrassed. But I put my hand into the black handkerchief and took out two pennies, they were all pennies. 'Now have a biscuit,' the other one said. So I did. I took it, and ate it. And they watched me very closely, smiling and eager, as though waiting to see if I'd learned the lesson. Then they walked out, offering pennies and biscuits to other people.

MACEY: It makes me very angry.

SIMONE: Why, Macey?

MACEY: Cosy masks! Imposed personalities! Silly little minds.

SIMONE: But they like our shops.

MACEY: All right, so they possess a sweet-natured grubbiness, but they're still susceptible to loud-mouthed culture and political fraudulence. It irritates me.

SIMONE: What's irritating about the young is that we're not.

MACEY: Maybe. I'm reaching the age where I employ a desperate charm in order to gain the attention of all those lovely young girls whose silly little minds I despise. And the price I pay for this flattery is to listen to their dull thoughts offered with shrill immodest modesty, you know? – hiding their conceits trying to be humble? Terrible age, really; the age where I only want to hurt, give pain, make others suffer. A sour age.

> *Suddenly MANFRED, carrying a tray of coffee and toast in one hand, drags ROLAND in with the other.*
>
> *ROLAND is struggling to put on a shirt through which blood is seeping.*
>
> *SIMONE stifles a scream. He has been cutting his body with a razor and rubbing salt into it.*

MANFRED: Look what I found this bloody fool doing.

> *ESTHER sits up but cannot see what has happened and MANFRED immediately goes to distract her.*
>
> *The others move in to ROLAND.*

ROLAND: *(Hissing whisper.)* Don't! Leave me.

ESTHER: Did I hear a scream?

ROLAND: And don't tell her anything.

SIMONE: It's nothing, Kitten. I broke a glass, a little cut.

> *SIMONE bends pretending to pick up something.*
>
> *TESSA takes a towel to cover ROLAND's shoulders.*
>
> *ROLAND enters deeper into the room and sits on a stool, tense from his self-inflicted pain.*

ESTHER: Why is Roland in a towel? Roland – why are you in a towel?

SIMONE: He's just washed his hair.

> *ROLAND pathetically rubs his hair.*

MANFRED: I'm sorry the coffee took so long, Ketzel.

ESTHER: You know, there was a doctor who discovered he had leukaemia because one day he bought a new microscope and tested it by looking at a sample of his own blood.

TESSA: *(To ROLAND.)* What have you done?

CRISPIN: Razor cuts, they're razor cuts.

MANFRED: *(To ESTHER.)* The blood-count was improved last week, my kitten, so they must have found the right drug for you.

ROLAND: Tell me she's not suffering.

TESSA: What good do you think those cuts are doing, fool, what good?

ESTHER: *(To MANFRED.)* You know how *I* knew? Roland was making love to me one night and asked me, 'Where did you get those bruises from?' 'What bruises?' I asked him. 'Those ones,' he said, 'there, and there, and there and there and there.'

CRISPIN: And salt. He rubbed them in with salt.

ROLAND: Stop staring at me. Go away. She'll see you.

SIMONE: Let me sponge you.

ROLAND: Don't come near me. I want to share the pain. I've never had any pain in my life. Please God make it hurt more and perhaps she won't die.

TESSA: Fool!

> *As he talks, ROLAND rubs the salt deeper into his wounds.*

> *In the frozen silence ESTHER becomes suspicious.*

ESTHER: What is it? Why is everyone standing around? I know what it is. Its depression time again. I'm dying and you want me to make it easier for you by pretending I'm not, isn't it? Come on now, we're all too clever for deceits and denials. And what's more they make my misery worse. Much, much worse. MACEY! I want to go on living! ROLAND! I *don't* want to die. MANFRED, SIMONE, TESSA! All of you. I-do-not-want-to-die.

> *Pause and distress.*

My God, that was cruel of me, wasn't it. Forgive me, everyone, take no notice. I didn't mean to give you pain.

TESSA: *(Low and fierce to ROLAND.)* Fool, fool, fool.

ESTHER: Yes, I did. I did mean to give pain. I should say I don't mind, make it easier for you, but I do – I do – I just do.

> *Long pause.*

Manfred I want to walk. Help me.

> *She rises, talking, MANFRED helping.*

Do you know anybody who was prepared to die? Despite all the suffering and the knowledge of suffering and man's inhumanity, everyone wants to go on living – for ever and ever, gloriously.

> *She takes a stick and slowly circles the room, touching, remembering.*

Some people of course know that when they're old they'll become tired and ready to go; or else they grow to despise themselves so much for not being what they thought they were that they become eager to fade out. Not me, though. I can't tell you how much I cherish everything. I know there's a lot that's obscene and ugly but it's never been too oppressive. *You* know that, don't you, Roland? In the end there's such sweetness, such joy in hidden places. I want to stay on and not miss anything. I want to stay with you, all of you, close and warm and happy. Why shouldn't I want that? And think – all those things I haven't done. Every year the world finds something new to offer me: another man makes music or carves an impossible shape out of the rocks or sings us a poem. Someone is always rising up, taking wing, and behind him he pulls the rest of us; and I want to be there, for every movement, every sound. Why should I want to die away from all that?

> *ESTHER falters, CRISPIN goes to her.*

That's made me tired again, that has.

> *She returns to her bed, exhausted.*

I keep wanting to talk and I keep getting tired. Manfred, take the pillows away.

> *ESTHER slides into bed eyes closed.*

> *SIMONE moves to MANFRED who has left ESTHER's bedside, desolate, unable to contain his anguish. She clasps him in her arms.*

TESSA: *(To CRISPIN.)* Hold me, Crispin, just this last time, I'll not ask thee again.

> *She clasps him but his response betrays reluctance.*

> *MACEY, disturbed, and despite himself, is drawn to ROLAND.*

> *MACEY, unable to believe he could ever bring himself to do it, gently sponges ROLAND's back.*

MACEY: Children, you're all children. Leave each other alone. It's not right, you don't know what you're doing, any of you.

> *End scene.*

SCENE TWO

> *Three hours have passed. Dinner has been eaten.*
>
> *ESTHER sleeps.*
>
> *MANFRED lies on top of the blankets close to her.*
>
> *SIMONE sews buttons on a shirt.*
>
> *MACEY has remained. He is a little drunk.*

MACEY: Why don't I go?

> *(Pause.)*

(To SIMONE.) There's a great stillness in you, girl. I've never known anyone to radiate such calm. How can you be so still in such a restless house?

> *(Pause.)*

Why don't I go?

SIMONE: Stay, Macey. There's no shop tomorrow. Help us kill Sunday.

MACEY: Look at him, Manfred, there. He won't leave her alone. He can't hold on *for* her. *(Pause.)* I've drunk too much. Everyone's crawled into some corner of the house and no one's said anything to me and I don't know what I'm supposed to do. *(Beat.)* How can you be so still?

SIMONE: Everyone asks that. It's not stillness, really, it's a protective silence. If I say or do too much I'm always afraid someone will stamp on me.

MACEY: That lot'd miss you for a start –

SIMONE: That's just because I'm so desperate to be wanted.

MACEY: – cuddling their tempers when their arses need kicking.

SIMONE: They're lucky, the others.

MACEY: Why don't I go?

SIMONE: The same art college up north, same kind of labouring fathers and tight-lipped mothers.

MACEY: Ha! Labouring fathers and tight-lipped mothers. I like that.

SIMONE: And they built the shops for them.

MACEY: Only they never came.

SIMONE: My lot came instead.

MACEY: Not Crispin's driver dad nor Roland's religious floor-scrubbing mum.

SIMONE: But slim young actresses and architects' wives.

MACEY: Not Tessa's bricklaying brothers.

SIMONE: But politicians' daughters.

MACEY: *(Indicating MANFRED and ESTHER.)* Not even their parents: The Leeds Jewish Anarchists' Association – ten hours a day stitching linings; no furniture and all books.

SIMONE: And you know, Macey, it's broken their hearts.

MACEY: I know it.

> *MANFRED comes forward. He seems in a trance.*

MANFRED: How strange.

MACEY: So you were awake then?

MANFRED: I think I've been dreaming.

MACEY: Oh, so you weren't awake then?

MANFRED: But I wasn't asleep.

MACEY: So you *were* awake then!

MANFRED: I have a powerful urge to say something. As though I've been instructed, as though I've had an epiphany.

MACEY: Epiphany. Wonderful word.

MANFRED: But I can't bring myself to say it. It sounds so banal. And yet lying there it seemed profound, urgent. Even now I feel – don't laugh – possessed. By Esther. By her words. I want to say *(Struggling.)* we must be honest. That's all. Just four words. All of a sudden – We, I must be honest. Who do *I* hate, who do *I* love, who do I value, who do I despise, what pleases *me*, what offends *me*? Esther's questions. And I want to ask everybody: what offends *them*? That's why revolutions happen, isn't it? – something offends. Macey, you, why are you a manager?

MACEY: I should've gone.

MANFRED: You manage other men's affairs, you don't create or invent or produce but you manage what other men produce. Why? A man who loves words. Why?

MACEY: Simone, Manfred – good night to you.

MANFRED: Esther's dying, Macey. We're growing old bit by bit. Every word is a second, passing. It'll never return, never. I shall never be young again. I shall never laugh the same way again. I shall never love for the first time again, never discover my first sight of the sea, nor stumble across literature, never. I'll reach out to recapture or remember – but that first ecstasy of all things? Never again. So, it's important. I *must* know. What do I really love? What do I dare to say I despise?

Long pause.

Englishmen! I despise the Englishman. Belief embarrasses him.

Pause.

Is that all I wanted to say?

Trying again.

Belief demands passion, and passion terrifies him, renders him vulnerable so he believes in nothing. He's not terrified of action. Action, battles, defeats – they're easy for him. No, it's ridicule. Passion invites ridicule; men wither from that. Listen to an Englishman talk, there's no real sweetness there, no simplicity, only sneers. The love sneer, the political sneer, the religious sneer – sad.

Pause.

Stirs himself.

Macey's right. We must sell the shop, not fold it up. Sell it and start again, something else. I want to talk about it. Simone, call Tessa and Crispin, drag Roland out from wherever he's crawled – we'll talk, plot. It's so long since we've plotted.

Long pause.

Terrible, isn't it. I can't bring myself to believe any of that. Lying there it sounded so logical and right; but saying it, actually mouthing the words 'we must be honest' – nothing. Stale.

> *MANFRED returns to his model, adding to it unenthusiastically.*

SIMONE: Manfred, can *I* say something to you – ?

MANFRED: I don't think so, Simone … Thanks, but – forget it.

* * *

SIMONE: Play me a game of chess, Macey. Keep me company.

MACEY: I must go.

SIMONE: I'm not very good, you can beat me.

MACEY: Why don't I go?

SIMONE: Here. *(Indicates eighteenth-century chair.)* Sit here.

MACEY: Now.

SIMONE: Beautiful chair, isn't it?

MACEY: Before the others return.

SIMONE: I know other people's pain is a trap, but stay – I beg
you. Look, look at these chessmen. Crispin made them,
he's made the king like Don Quixote, and Sancho Panza is
the Queen trying to protect him.

> *They play.*
>
> *While they are playing, ROLAND enters with 'paper'
> burning in his fingers. He brings it to an ashtray and
> watches it burn.*
>
> *MACEY is incredulous realizing what it is.*

MACEY: That's money!

ROLAND: Watch.

> *Takes another pound note and burns it.*

Look at it. What does it make you feel?

> *MACEY, unable to control himself, stamps it out.*

So? What've you saved? Does it make you feel better now?
You should do it. Take a pound note from your wallet and
burn it. Try. Look, I'll do it again. Watch.

> *MACEY is mesmerized as ROLAND burns another.*

The last time I did that was in a restaurant with Esther. She cried.

MACEY: I could never do that, never.

ROLAND: You don't know, try it.

MACEY: With hunger in the world I know it without even trying.

> *SIMONE, realising she's lost MACEY, reaches for the shirt and continues sewing on buttons.*

SIMONE: You're cheating, aren't you, Roland. Three pound notes? Nothing more?

ROLAND: You're right, of course. Such little gestures for big angers. Aaaah!

SIMONE: Your back?

ROLAND: If only I didn't have to move. Pain needs contemplation.

> *ROLAND takes up his Yoga position.*

It's irritating otherwise. Irritation – so petty.

> *TESSA and CRISPIN return.*

> *He is in a vicious mood, waving a letter at SIMONE.*

CRISPIN: Another one.

TESSA: Crispin, no!

CRISPIN: I've found another one. Wherever I go I find thy notes waiting for me, like an ambush. In t'pockets, under t'pillows, on t'deck – everywhere. Tha even posts 'em to me. We live in the same house and tha posts me letters. Tha little mad girl, thee, why dast dae't?

TESSA: Crispin, please, leave her alone.

CRISPIN: An' what in hell is't tha' doing that for? Can't I sew my own buttons? Look at her! Look at that ancient, Gothic face. Full of apology for belonging to her class. Do you knoa how she sees us, Macey? As working-class heroes bringing light and beauty to our mums and brothers. Stop looking so sad for me.

SIMONE: All right, I promise, never again, but no more scenes.

CRISPIN: Nay, I'm not ower finished yet.

SIMONE: So cruel. You're so cruel and unsubtle.

CRISPIN: What's subtlety got to do wi' anything? She misuses words and emotions like an illiterate office girl.

SIMONE: All right, I'm hurt, you've succeeded. Don't go on.

CRISPIN: Listen to this: *(Reading from letter.)* 'Oh my darling. Instinctively I sense a crisis in your soul.' A crisis in my soul! That's how subtle she is. 'Do not evade my glances of concern.' And how's that for a fat platitude? 'Glances of concern.' And I have to read it, every day. Words pour out of her. What do any of them mean? 'Oh my dearest I feel all your depths of pain and difficulty'. Where dast find time to write such great nonsense? 'But you choose to insult me as if my natural interest to communicate at such times was wrong and ugly and I feel like an old jar of marmalade left to mildew…'

> *The last words bring CRISPIN to a slow halt as the pain of SIMONE's letters reaches him through that last poignant image. Ashamed, he retreats from her.*
>
> *TESSA tries to comfort SIMONE.*

SIMONE: Forgive me, Tessa. I couldn't keep it to myself all the time. I thought I could give him strength, ?

TESSA: It's all right, don't go on. I don't mind.

SIMONE: You do, I know it. I can feel it in the way you touch me.

> *TESSA moves to be near CRISPIN.*

Oh God, I feel so rejected, I can't bear it. There's such pain in this house.

The FRIENDS are a tableau of misery and silence.

They have known each other most of their lives.

ROLAND: I always think that while a *good* man sins or acts out some wretched piece of misery or offends his own gentleness, God turns away and doesn't look and tactfully leaves him alone to do it in private. That's a good world, that one, with a Good God. It consoles me, that. Doesn't make it easier to bear, but it's kinder.

End Scene.

SCENE THREE

Some hours later. About 2 a.m.

MANFRED is reading at his desk and making more notes.

ROLAND is sitting beside ESTHER's bed and reading to her from Djuna Barnes's Nightwood.

SIMONE is by now drunk.

MACEY sleeps in a chair.

CRISPIN plays chess with himself.

TESSA sits at his feet strumming a guitar.

ROLAND: 'Nora had the face of all the people who love the people – a face that would be evil when she found out that to love without criticism is to be betrayed... Those who love everything are despised by everything, as those...

ESTHER: No more, Roland. Manfred, help me, I want to walk out into the room.

MANFRED: No, Ketzel, stay resting. We'll come to you if you want.

ROLAND: Let her walk.

ESTHER: I want to stretch and move.

ROLAND: Let her if she wants to.

ESTHER: You should be glad, shouldn't he, Roland?

ROLAND: She wants to step out and be alive. Come on, Kitten, ignore him.

> *Everyone rises to move things out of her way as ROLAND and MANFRED guide, like a queen, this pale and dying beauty to a stately chair.*
>
> *SIMONE places a low, soft stool under her feet.*
>
> *ESTHER is adored by them.*

ESTHER: Come on, Manfred, you're dying to tell us what you've been reading about. We're all ready.

> *MANFRED picks up his papers and, with mock seriousness, begins to read through his notes as though recounting a thriller.*
>
> *It is of paramount importance that the actor makes as much sense of this précis as possible while at the same time clowning the story.*

MANFRED: You all thought there were only social revolutions, the French, the industrial and the Russian, eh? Well you're wrong. I've got others just as epoch-making. Listen to this. This book tells that in 1600 a man called Gilbert, who was the personal physician to Queen Elizabeth the First, wrote a 'famous' book called *De Magnete,* about an electroscope which, three centuries later, turned out to be *'indispensible* to the development of physical science' and which enabled a man called Thompson to discover that electricity was made of particles which he called electrons, and this discovery had 'the most *profound* effect on physical science'. 'Profound!' 'Indispensible!' 1897! Revolution number one!

And then an American physicist called Millikan measured the electric charge of an electron which led to the *extraordinary* conclusion that its mass was 1/1835 of an hydrogen atom and thus demonstrated that particles even *smaller* than atoms existed. Revolution number two – 'extraordinary'.

Next, a few years later, the Curies! Radium! The nature of radioactivity revealed! And what was its nature? Within it, atoms spontaneously exploded! Out went radiation while behind was left – a new atom! – thus showing that the immutability of the elemental atoms was a myth and so 'twentieth-century science was launched on its fateful journey into the *restless world* of the atom'. That was the third revolution. 'A restless world'.

Now – it gets even more exciting – a man called Max Planck developed a theory called the quantum theory which said that radiant heat was a discontinuous mass made up of particles and *not* smooth waves, and that was 'so revolutionary' that even its originator didn't believe it! Einstein had to prove him right drawing conclusions which were *themselves* revolutionary – because he applied Planck's ideas with 'devastating results to the photo-electric effect and discovered that light itself also consisted of multitudes of individual parcels of energy and not waves'. 'Physicists were incredulous'! Is says so here. 'Devastating... incredulous'. *(Taps book.)* Numbers four and five.

But that was nothing, because Einstein then went on not to the sixth revolution but to a revolutionary concept of the very nature of revolutions. 'A revolutionary concept about the nature of revolutions. He shook the hitherto unshakeable concepts of physic with his famous theory of relativity which, as we all know, has the central principle that all natural phenomena are subject to the same laws for an observer moving at speed as they are for an another observer moving at another speed. If you went on a trip in space you'd return to find your twin brother older than yourself. 'Common sense mocked' cried the headlines.

But man cannot live by theories alone. While the theorists were theorizing, the experimentalists were experimenting. Back to the atom. Beginning in Manchester and ending in Cambridge a man called Rutherford, following in the footsteps of Thompson who, you will remember discovered the electron, pursued experiments into the nature of the atom which, he found, was essentially empty! All that was there was a nucleus of miniscule size and gargantuan density in which all the atom's mass was concentrated with electrons orbiting like planets round the sun. Another revolution is taking shape.

Inspired by Rutherford, a Dane called Niels Bohr applied quantum theory to the behaviour of electrons inside of atoms in order to understand how light was born. 'And God said "let there be light," and all the little atoms spat out light. The revolutions shape on.

Not without difficulty however. Bohr was unable to find the spectra for complicated atoms and he couldn't account for the behaviour of extra nuclear electrons in any but the simplest of atoms. Now his failure became another man's challenge, a young German physicist in 1924 called Werner Heisenberg, at the tender age of twenty-three set out to invent a mathematical theory which would account for the spectral lines which could be observed. But – also in 1924 – unknown to Heisenberg who was courageously going forward – Louis de Broglie of Paris was going all the way back. 'Light is waves,' he said to everyone. 'No, light is particles' had said Einstein. 'Electrons are grains of matter,' had said Thompson. 'No,' de Broglie now said, 'they're trains of waves.' No revolution is without its problems! The thrilling microscopic world of the atom refused to behave in the same way as the mediocre macroscopic world of man. It was not the same as planets round the sun, and along came an Austrian physicist called Erwin Schrodinger to demonstrate it.

Based on de Broglie's conjecture Schrodinger evolved an entirely new mathematical approach specifically designed to describe the behaviour of this incredible miniature world. Revolutions within revolutions! But – young Heisenberg was not satisfied with merely a mathematical description of the dual nature of the electron and so, in 1927, like Einstein – but in a different context – he revised the fundamental meaning of physical measurement. No less! Heisenberg asked: how does one know anything about atomic particles? To what extent can we measure them? Can you measure their properties? The analysis of the microscopic nature of the atomic world was such that it drove him to introduce an extraordinary principle which is called 'the principle of uncertainty' which states this: 'that in the nature of things it is impossible to specify the exact position and exact velocity of an electron at the same minute; the uncertainty in the position could be decreased only by increasing the uncertainty in the speed or vice-versa;' and guess what – the product of the two uncertainties turned out to be a simple multiple of Planck's constant! *'Revised fundamental meaning! Extraordinary principle! Of uncertainty!*

'Of course, Heisenberg's uncertainty doesn't affect the behaviour of the world in the gross. The sun is always there, an hour remains an hour, seeds become wheat, babies grow into adults, but its transformation of the fine detail from an exact and predictable pattern into a blur of probabilities was yet another major revolution in scientific thought!

ESTHER: Wait a minute, wait a minute. 'its transformation from an exact and predictable pattern into a blur of possibilities was a major revolution in scientific thought'?

MANFRED: Precisely.

ESTHER: Moving from a *predictable* pattern into a *blur* represented *a major revolution in thought?*

Freely-like an improvisation

We've bur-ied the win - ter mar-ried the spring, and now we have a time to pause and think a-gain and sing We've plant-ed seeds grant-ed birds their songs, now we have a time to rest and right a-gain those wrongs,

TOGETHER:

Chorus *(faster)*

If there's a heart in you, a part of you that can re - lent re - live for - get for - give then

(slower) *(faster)*

cov-er wounds I've gi - ven you for wounds are wounds and

(slower)

words are words and no a-mount of cry-ing cry-ing

(slower) *(faster)*

cov-ers them or heals them Live with them

(slowing down) *(slower)*

Live with them Live with them.

MANFRED: I kid you not! But wait – the revolution has yet to reach its climax. 1930!

Enter a Cambridge mathematician called P.A.M. Dirac. He synthesizes the physical ideas of Planck, Heisenberg, de Broglie and Schrodinger, fits them into the framework of Einstein's theory of relativity and low and behold – a book called Relativistic Quantum Mechanics in which undreamt of phenomena were revealed. *Undreamt* of! Such as the creation and annihilation of particles and antiparticles. It was, this author says 'an epoch-making book'. Epoch-making! And have we read it? And all those revolutions – have we heard about them? And that was only up to 1930, there's another forty years to go! And my God! What shall we do?

ESTHER: You will grow bald and become blind and I have no patience with you any longer.

TESSA: *(To a guitar.)*

The leaves are turning,

The earth has turned,

And now there is a time for burning

Hates we left

Unburned.

The year's beginning,

Long nights will sow

Soft seeds for those softer days

The wrong ways

Must go.

TOGETHER: If there's a heart in you …

ESTHER: Simone, stop drinking.

SIMONE: I'm not drunk. What does it matter?

MACEY: *(Who has slowly woken up during the song.)* Jesus! What a head I've got. What time is it? Two-thirty in the morning, lunacy! Argh! My mouth's like starch washing day.

ESTHER: Simone, give Macey a long cool drink. Relax, Macey. It's the best time of night. I don't even feel tired.

MACEY: You just don't leave each other alone.

ESTHER: Feel this room, Macey. Quiet, friendly – it's a gentle room, this, nothing can touch us here –

MACEY: You think not?

ESTHER: Isn't that so, Manfred? Manfred! What's he doing now?

MANFRED: The appeals, Ketzel – I forgot to sign the cheques.

MACEY: The what?

ESTHER: You didn't know, did you, Macey, that Manfred forced us all to agree that one-third of our profits should go to help the third world?

MACEY: What profits, for God's sake? Am I in a madhouse or something?

ESTHER: Not charities, nor cancer research or ex-prisoners, nothing marginal like that. Revolution, Macey: arms for South Africa, medical supplies for North Vietnam, funds for guerrillas in Latin America, books for Cuba.

CRISPIN: It should be medical supplies.

SIMONE: *(Savagely.)* Makes you feel more humanitarian, doesn't it?

CRISPIN: *(Imploring.)* Simone!

ESTHER: The third world, Macey. We're all frightened of it. Our parents left us a heritage of colonial and racial bitterness and the third world hated them and is going to make us pay for it, and so we're all frightened.

MANFRED: Hatred is only an expediency, Ketzel.

ESTHER: Such a gentle person, my brother. Other people's need to hate makes such sense to him. That's why he forgives and tolerates rabble-rousers. Not me. Rabble-rousers frighten me, they're only rebels, not revolutionaries. My brother's a rebel, Macey, I – am a revolutionary.

MACEY: I don't understand.

ESTHER: My brother is a rebel because he hates the past, I'm a revolutionary because I see the past as too rich with human suffering and achievement to be dismissed. Women are natural revolutionaries, aren't they, Simone? Men are only ever rebels, their angers are negative, tiny, they *enjoy* the violence of opposing capitalism.

MACEY: Strange energies you all have. How can you concern yourselves with so much?

ESTHER: Macey thinks I'm teasing, Manfred; tell him it's only because I'm so wretchedly ill that I sound like teasing. Tell him.

> *ESTHER closes her eyes.*

> *CRISPIN wanders round the room, touching things, as though drugged.*

SIMONE: Crispin! You look like a zombie.

CRISPIN: Don't shout at me, Simone. No retaliations now. Peace, pax, pace, pace.

SIMONE: You're tender when *you* like, aren't you?

CRISPIN: Sssh. No little revenges, pace, pace, pace.

SIMONE: *(Mocking.)* Pace, pace, pace!

> *Silence; out of which grows a contrapuntal duologue between MANFRED and CRISPIN.*

> *MANFRED whispers to MACEY while CRISPIN talks to the others.*

CRISPIN: We've chosen good colours, gentle colours.

MANFRED: *(Coming down to confide in MACEY.)* *I* know what I
despise.

CRISPIN: There's so much suffering in the world – I need to
know about sweetness and light to soothe it all out.

MANFRED: I know but I daren't say it.

CRISPIN: The colours soothe me.

MANFRED: I've been feeling it for years.

CRISPIN: Is that wrong? To want to be soothed?

MANFRED: Even now, as I'm talking, I'm having difficulty
wrapping words round those feelings.

> *Pause.*

CRISPIN: Roland –

MANFRED: Hate them –

CRISPIN: Kiss me.

> *ROLAND and CRISPIN kiss each other on the lips and
> remain thus clasped during MANFRED's next words.*

MANFRED: *(Whispering almost.)* The working class! Hate them!
Despise them! My class – offend me.

> *CRISPIN breaks away from ROLAND to take TESSA
> in his arms, rocking her, cradling her.*

Their cowardly acquiescence, their rotten ordinariness –
everything about them – hate them!

> *ROLAND lays his head in ESTHER's lap.*

CRISPIN: That's what I want to do – I've just realized.

MANFRED: *(Still whispering.)* Those endless dreary episodes of
'ordinary life' on television.

CRISPIN: I want to caress everything, comfort people, tell
them it'll be all right in the end.

MANFRED: And there sits the ordinary man, watching himself, pleased and dumbly recognizing.

CRISPIN: Cars going round corners?

MANFRED: 'Hey' he says, 'that's me that is'.

CRISPIN: Isn't that a violent noise?

MANFRED: Gladys, come and look, just like you and me and Jack and Gwen and Kate and bloody ordinary Sammy in the pub. No need to change then, is there? We're good enough to make telly about.'

CRISPIN: I can't bear violence any more, or the news about violence: death by fire, famine, earthquake, war.

MANFRED: And then his children watch; and slowly they begin living a copy, not of their parents' *real* life; but the tepid telly version others have made of their parents' real life.

CRISPIN: I can't bear the violence of speech.

MANFRED: Isn't that extraordinary?

CRISPIN: Ugly people with violent voices, violent images on street corners, violent prejudices – they all batter me.

MANFRED: But look what happens next, Macey.

CRISPIN: Me nerves – they're all frayed and battered.

MANFRED: Along comes a new generation of writers and they begin writing new episodes about the *children* – whose ordinariness has doubled because all they've had to look up to was the tepid telly version of their parents which the last generation of writers put on the screen.

> *SIMONE, isolated, is drawn to sit by CRISPIN and TESSA. CRISPIN offers the comfort of his arms to her so that his strength is given to both women.*

CRISPIN: Peace, I need peace.

MANFRED: And soon, Macey – you'll see, there'll be stories about *their* children and their children's children, and the characters on the screen will become more and more feeble –

CRISPIN: Peace and silence.

MANFRED: – and the more banal their utterances the more like real life it'll seem until one day the screen will just be blank, an electronic fog, and they'll sit there and accept it and say nothing.

CRISPIN: Blessed peace and silence.

MANFRED: All those people we loved –

CRISPIN: I promise you –

MANFRED: Sad, like disappointed lovers, all that love, lost.

CRISPIN: Auden was right – we must love one another, or die.

MANFRED: – and I've no energy, no appetite for new loves.

CRISPIN: Believe me.

MANFRED: Some men retained their appetites, enjoyed the complexity and still survived – all their life –

CRISPIN: – everything will be all right.

MANFRED: – amazed!

CRISPIN: It will –

MANFRED: Each moment – surprised!

CRISPIN: I promise you.

MANFRED: And finally – joyous! Joyous to be witness to it all. Lovely men they were, Macey, not sour and thorny like us, but eager, capable – splendid outrages.

CRISPIN: Peace –

MANFRED: Waste!

CRISPIN: – and silence.

MANFRED: That's what I really wanted to say.

CRISPIN: Blessed peace and silence.

MANFRED: We're too old to pretend.

> *Suddenly MANFRED stops speaking, his attention drawn to ROLAND, who is slowly rising away from ESTHER as though he has just discovered something dreadful.*

> *One by one they all turn to look at ROLAND and each of them knows – ESTHER is dead.*

ACT TWO

SCENE ONE

The same room. Some hours later.

The body of ESTHER lies under blankets.

ROLAND has gathered a number of her garments and laid them at the foot of her bed. He sits, gazing at the body, holding a jumper to his face.

SIMONE enters in a dressing-gown.

SIMONE: Roland?

ROLAND: She had an odour, faint, delicate.

SIMONE: Roland!

ROLAND: When I came into a room I knew she'd been there.

SIMONE: You ought to leave this room, Roland.

ROLAND: Not a perfume, nothing sweet or sickly, but the smell of movement, skin that had worked hard.

SIMONE: Would you like me to sponge you?

ROLAND: Please. I think so.

> *SIMONE pulls down his shirt, and slowly sponges.*
>
> *Referring to his self-immolation:*

You're not frightened of dying, are you?

SIMONE: No.

ROLAND: What will you do now?

SIMONE: I'd like to do just that: die, creep away and die. Give me a reason why not.

> *Silence.*

Roland?

ROLAND: Go back to bed, Simone. You've been drinking all
night.

SIMONE: Never mind that. Give me a reason why I shouldn't
do it now, get up and walk away and never come back.
(Pause.) You can't, can you?

ROLAND: I'm not the right person to ask.

SIMONE: You can't give me a reason, can you?

ROLAND: No, I can't. Please leave me alone now, Simone.

> *He takes up a simple Yoga sitting position and closes
> his eyes.*

SIMONE: *(Rising.)* You don't know what it's like to talk and not
be heard; to offer and not be taken; to be eager and not
needed. There's not a creature needs me, not one single
one, not really *need.* I feel so useless and dismissed. I just
want to creep away, pick myself up, and never come back.
I'd so love that.

> *SIMONE now regards ROLAND in his sitting position.*
>
> *Then, with great contempt:*

That's all nonsense, Roland. Lie in green fields if you want
peace, climb mountains or walk in forests if you want to
meditate. You won't come to terms with death in Yoga
squats.

> *He ignores her; she watches a few seconds longer then
> leaves. After she has gone ROLAND relaxes, opens his
> eyes, reaches for a garment into which he buries his
> face, then crumbles, miserably, into the folds covering
> the dead woman.*

SCENE TWO

Later.

ROLAND whimpering.

ROLAND: Take me with you, Esther. I don't really want to go on. I'm so tired and empty.

Silence.

MACEY enters. He's just emerged from trying to sleep, and is tucking his shirt into his trousers.

MACEY: I can't sleep in this house; you're whimpering all night and the others keep moving about. What the hell good do you think you're doing there, and those cuts all exposed? Put something over you, you bloody child, you.

He offers him a black pullover, which ROLAND ignores.

Leaves him to put on his tie in front of the mirror. Struggles agitatedly.

You're weird, all of you. And unnatural. Esther was the only healthy one of the lot of you. Just let the press get pictures of you all now. 'The Trend-makers'! Huh! The habit of discontent was all your lot ever created. Real class terrorists you were, intimidating everyone over the age of twenty-five with your swinging this and your swinging that. You never thought you'd grow old or die.

Here, let me help you. Look at you. They'll fester, those cuts. You must be wracked with pain. And put on a pullover, it's cold.

He helps the pathetically struggling ROLAND to put on the black pullover, then wanders miserably round the room.

This room is festering. With gloom. Restless bloody house.

Stops in front of MANFRED's model.

Questions! Suddenly everyone's full of heavyweight questions. 'Who do you really love, really hate? Why are you a manager?' Who asks such questions at my age? I know why I'm a manager, what good does it do me?

The atmosphere draws an answer from him.

Because each morning I wake up knowing that I don't love the woman at my side, and haven't done for the last fifteen years – that really defeats me. No love – no appetites. Even before the day begins I'm done.

Pause.

But I've managed.

Why, I ask myself, why *exactly* didn't I love her? Not a bad woman, very good in fact, even wise – about simple things – loyal, sense of humour – everybody loves her – except me; so why? You know why? Because *I* had the capacity to grow and *she* didn't. She grew, true, but, one day she stopped and I went on. Simple! And I had to accept that she was a reflection of me. At one time in my life my entire capacity to love was focused on her. She was what I needed. And I had to ask myself, 'Could I have had such small needs?' She reminds me, every day, that at one time in my life I had small needs. There! Honest confessions! But who's satisfied? No one! Because they don't tell me anything those honest confessions. What am I supposed to do with them, tell me, what?

ROLAND is trying to climb up alongside ESTHER.

What-are-you-doing-for-God's-sake? Get away from that body. Leave it alone!

MACEY in righteous anger pulls ROLAND violently to the floor, causing him great pain.

I'm sorry, son, I'm sorry.

ROLAND: No, no. It's good.

MACEY: Those cuts, I forgot those cuts.

ROLAND: Leave me, it's good I say. The pain, it's good, it's good, IT'S GOOD!

MACEY: You disgust me. *(Leaving.)* If you imagine you can overcome death by creeping up on it like that you're mistaken. And not all your silly self-inflicted pain will help either. One day you're going to die and that's that.

ROLAND: There's no such thing as death.

MACEY: Idiot!

ROLAND: Death doesn't exist.

MACEY: Mumbo jumbo! Idiot! IDIOT!

> *MACEY leaves.*

> *ROLAND creeps back to the garments and again smells them, desperately trying to recapture the living ESTHER.*

SCENE THREE

An hour later.

> *ROLAND is still at the foot of the bed. TESSA is at his side, trying to draw him away.*

TESSA: Roland, come on, sleep, lovely.

ROLAND: I'm really frightened now, Tessa, panicking.

TESSA: You've given yourself too much pain, lad. Shall I make you a cup of hot tea? Without milk? Some lemon and lots of brandy? Will that be nice?

ROLAND: That tight brain I had, all wrapped up with confidence – it's fallen apart. What do I do?

TESSA: Don't ask, Roland, please don't ask.

ROLAND: Panicking. I can feel it, Tess. Terror and panic.

TESSA: Come away.

ROLAND: When I die, where will it be? How will it happen? Will I know I'm dying? Will I lie there knowing everything and knowing I can't stop it?

TESSA: And you're tired.

ROLAND: I've run down, Tess. Look. Stopped. That was my last word.

> *He has said it, but only after he has said it does he realize it must be true, for now he opens his mouth to say something and cannot.*
>
> *Terror and panic show in his eyes.*

TESSA: Roland, stop it. It's not honest. You can't stop talking. It's not possible. Say 'Tessa', say that. 'Tessa, Tessa, Tessa.' Scream then. ROLAND!

> *ROLAND releases a sad and desperate moan and pitches his face into TESSA's lap. She rocks him and laments.*

Oh, my poor bewildered boy. We're none of us what we thought we were. But you shouldn't upset yourself. You upset us when you do that, and we need each other now so much.

> *She shakes him but he is in a catatonic state.*

Roland? Roland?

> *Abruptly she rises.*

Don't let his panic get you, Tessa, hold on.

> *She wanders around the room in a fever of distress, reaches for her guitar and smashes it against the eighteenth-century chair.*

Too late, Tess, too late.

> *CRISPIN enters to find the cause of the noise.*

CRISPIN: Tessa!

TESSA: Oh, Crispin!

Relieved, she clasps him in search of comfort – he cannot respond.

Aye, lad, too late.

She flees.

CRISPIN collects the pieces of her guitar and tucks them in a corner.

Then turns to ROLAND.

CRISPIN: Tha's frightened *now*, lad? Eh? Really frightened. And I can't comfort thee, nor thee me, nor any of us t'other.

ROLAND shrinks.

CRISPIN kneels, takes him in his arms and kisses him as he would an unhappy child.

Aye, I'll tak thee in me arms and gi' thee kindness but there's nowt of comfort in me. (Pause) Shall I tell thee what I do, lad? Will that ease thy misery a bit?

I sleep wi' owld ladies, me. I discovered one day they like me and they want me and I can gi' mesen to them. I can rouse owld passions wi' me lips and me hands and a lot of gentleness – like raising the dead. But they want to pay me and I take the money and the pleasure on it turns to shame and disgust and I swear I'll not touch them again but I do. Unnatural passions! Denys me the right of saying owt to any man.

Pause.

It's a good dialect, ours, ent it, Roland? We've noan on us got it still but it's a good, rich dialect from your smoky north. I think I'll keep it by me.

Aye, tha's taken it badly, lad. And it's not ower yet. The morning'll bring its tempers, eh? Its snapping and snarling. We'll kick each other before t'day's through, that's for sure.

Rocking, rocking.

Fade.

SCENE FOUR

Morning.

TESSA, MANFRED, CRISPIN, SIMONE, MACEY and ROLAND are ranged in different corners of the room:

SIMONE, more isolated from the rest, is still in her dressing-gown;

ROLAND, huddled against the side of the bed, is dressed as in the previous scene;

MACEY is sunk in the wing-backed armchair, his suit crumpled now. The rest are dressed in black.

MANFRED sits by his desk.

CRISPIN fiddles with his 'toy' by the window.

TESSA, back to the audience, stands hugging herself in the centre of the room.

TESSA: You look awful, Simone. Go away and dress.

SIMONE leaves.

Silence.

Oh, I feel so old this year and not very wise.

MACEY: Well, and what are you going to do now?

TESSA: What's left worth the while to do, Macey?

MACEY: What a rag-bag of shabby doubts you lot are.

MANFRED: Don't fight.

MACEY: *(Mocking.)* "What's left worth the while to do, Macey?"

MANFRED: Please.

MACEY: So thin, your question, so feeble and thin.

MANFRED: *(Moving to sit by the bed.)* Please, please don't fight.

MACEY: And when are you going to bury her? Can't be a Jewish cemetery, Manfred, you don't belong to a synagogue.

Pause.

TESSA: *(To CRISPIN.)* We've no children, that's what it is. Too frightened to make babies, weren't we? They would bind us. Too beautiful, too important to be bound down. Dead lovelies, us.

Pause.

Takes toy from CRISPIN.

Toys you made. For other people's kids. The nearest *you* got to paternal instincts.

Returns toy.

SIMONE returns.

Somehow, with the exception of ROLAND and MACEY, the positions of each shift into a pattern where SIMONE is left isolated and the others seem ranged against her.

SIMONE senses this, the others not.

SIMONE: So, the mistress is dead and I'm the first to go.

The others are caught off balance with this perception by SIMONE of what they are forced to realize was their subconscious feeling.

TESSA: What does that nonsense mean?

SIMONE: You know very well what it means.

TESSA: You have a knack for making people feel what they don't feel simply by suspecting them of feeling it.

CRISPIN: She's such a sensitive, delicate soul.

SIMONE: It's not nice what you're all doing now, not just.

CRISPIN: 'Nice'! Such an indifferent word: 'nice'.

SIMONE: I'll go then.

TESSA: Oh stop it, Simone. Can't you understand for once?

SIMONE: And can't I be understood for once?

CRISPIN: Is she complaining about being rejected now?

SIMONE: Talk to *me*, Crispin. I'm in the room, I've got a name.

CRISPIN: If I talk to her directly she'll think I'm in love with her.

SIMONE: You're very cruel, you, with your 'pace, pace'

TESSA: And stop your upper-class whining.

SIMONE: I'm sorry about my upper-class tone, but I don't feel *less* because I come from an upper-class family. We've got past that surely, Tessa?

TESSA: Well we haven't, so there! My father's a railwayman and yours is a company director and nothing can change that.

SIMONE: *(Hardly daring.)* Except the fact that *you're* a company director.

MACEY: Ah ha! She has fight. That stings doesn't it, Tess!

SIMONE: Oh, Macey! It's all so unworthy.

TESSA: TAKE HER AWAY! Go, Simone, for God's sake, go. Go and maybe by some miracle this room'll go with you. Out – get out, out – out – OUT!

> *Long pause.*

Oh, Simone. I'm sorry. You know we don't mean it. It's shock; Esther's dead and suddenly we're old and we're none of us what we thought we were.

> *Pause.*

Oh dear mother, what's happened to me? I used to be a joke for you all, I used to get angry to make you laugh, that was my role. No laughter now, just a croak, and I can't get rid of it. Christ! I wish I was a girl again.

Pause

MANFRED: There is about us all such a great poverty of intention.

* * *

CRISPIN: Simone, I'm sorry if I –

SIMONE: I don't care for the sound of your voice just now, Crispin.

CRISPIN: I want to apologize, make peace.

SIMONE: You only want to make peace because you've discovered a need for old women and you disgust yourself.

TESSA: SIMONE!

SIMONE: He won't give *us* his favours because he sells them.

TESSA: Shut up!

SIMONE: Can't be harsh on the world now, can you? Guilt's drained your moral energy.

MANFRED: 'Thus conscience doth make cowards of us all'.

CRISPIN: I found this need.

SIMONE: Tenderness?

CRISPIN: Old women, lovely sad old women. I could make girls of them.

TESSA: You rejected, sour bitch, you.

CRISPIN: But Simone's right. How can you guide anyone anywhere when such a passion destroys your credentials?

TESSA: Have pity on yourself, Crispin. There's no shame there.

SIMONE: I didn't want to shame you, Crispin.

TESSA: Oh you've taken on a great responsibility now, Simone.

SIMONE: I'll give you tenderness, Crispin.

TESSA and CRISPIN turn away.

Macey, help me.

MACEY: How? Help you, how?

SIMONE: They started it, not me.

MACEY: *(To TESSA.)* Is that all you've got courage for? Bury Esther!

SIMONE: They think I'm a silly, little bourgeois girl.

MACEY: At a time like this you turn on Simone? Esther, bury Esther.

An attack is now gathering force from SIMONE and MACEY.

* * *

SIMONE: Look at them! Jumped-up downcast proles –

MACEY: – evolving their little panaceas and getting depressed because their mums and dads didn't share their tastes.

SIMONE: Why should your labouring fathers and tight-lipped mothers come to the shops anyway?

MACEY: What of the world's problems would that've solved?

SIMONE: They think I can't tell them anything.

CRISPIN: She's been drinking all night.

SIMONE: So what if I've been drinking. Alcohol gives me purpose. You've needed me and I've worked and loved you all and I know what matters.

TESSA: What matters, Simone? Tell us.

SIMONE is caught off balance but struggles for a reply.

> *Unfortunately her terror of them makes her inaudible, she cannot even look at them, and uses MACEY as a conduit.*

SIMONE: Manfred shouldn't despise the working class.

TESSA: What was that?

SIMONE: And Crispin shouldn't be ashamed of his passion.

TESSA: I can't hear her, can you?

SIMONE: And Roland should stop hopping from one cult to another.

TESSA: What matters, Simone? We're waiting.

SIMONE: Justice.

TESSA: What did she say?

SIMONE: *(Still barely audible.)* I said 'justice' – and the pursuit of happiness.

TESSA: But what's she mumbling for?

MACEY: She said 'justice and the pursuit of happiness', that's what she said.

TESSA: *(Incredulously.)* But what has that got to do with anything?

MACEY: Well give her a chance. Tell them, Simone.

> *SIMONE is petrified by now and continues mumbling into MACEY as though he was her translator. She is clumsy and touching and pathetic.*

SIMONE: What I want to tell them is that order matters because –

TESSA: What's she saying now?

MACEY: She's saying order matters also, now quiet.

CRISPIN: 'Order'?

TESSA: It's becoming a nightmare.

SIMONE: Tell them order is not uniformity or sameness. Tell them you can make order out of different things.

TESSA: For God's sake tell it to us, Simone. Mumbling away in that old granny's ear.

SIMONE: I'm just saying that order doesn't necessarily lead to uniformity or sameness.

TESSA: Yes –

SIMONE: And that you can make order out of different things.

TESSA: Yes – and so?

SIMONE: Well don't you see? There's a difference between the order that paralyses and the order that liberates.

TESSA: Yes –

SIMONE: And that's what we're looking for, isn't it? The possibility of infinite variety? Isn't that –

CRISPIN: Noble?

SIMONE: Yes! Noble! So many blossomings. Noble! And what's more – there's room for failure when you've got order, and for weaknesses and – and –

CRISPIN: And everyman's fallibility?

SIMONE: Yes, Crispin. Everyman's fallibility.

CRISPIN: She's mad. She's been drinking all night and she's mad.

SIMONE: Oh, Crispin, isn't there anything in my madness touches you? Don't I deserve a little love for such loving madness?

MANFRED: *(Tenderly.)* Not now, Simone, not at this moment.

SIMONE: Yes, now, Manfred. Please let me go on.

MANFRED: It's all wrong to go on like this.

TESSA: And irrelevant.

MACEY: Let her talk, Tessa.

TESSA: But she's talking about order and nobility, and Esther's lying there dead and it's all irrelevant. Like this room, look at this lovely order we've cluttered ourselves with. Dead and ancient riches. And now we're trapped, hung up by them all.

> *She violently tips over the eighteenth-century chair.*
>
> *SIMONE rushes to rescue it.*

SIMONE: You should love it.

TESSA: *Love it?*

SIMONE: Memory, the past, signs of human activity – you should cherish them – I adore this room.

CRISPIN: Millions starving and we've surrounded ourselves with…

SIMONE: …with what? A few antiques from the past? Would they feed starving millions? More little gestures? Look at this chair. *(Points to the eighteenth-century chair.)* It's got to be somewhere, it can't be everywhere. Is the man who *wants* it and *has* it near him for most of the time a thief? Does wanting necessarily imply theft? … After all, what does him 'wanting' that chair mean? It could mean that he is responding to fine craftsmanship, to beauty.

MACEY: That's bad? That's immoral?

SIMONE: Don't you see the silly confusions you've got yourselves into?

TESSA: The apple doesn't fall far from the tree, does it?

CRISPIN: Class! What did you expect?

TESSA: Not dead yet.

MACEY: Ah ha! Class! Class, class, class! And what a mess your lot made of that issue. I'll handle this one, Simone! The working class is deprived, you said, 'stunted growth' you cried; 'promises unfulfilled'. And then – now listen to this – what did they do? They defended those same stunted growths, called them working-class values, applauded them, and then attacked bourgeois values as decadent. So tell me this, you idiots, you: if bourgeois values were only decadent and working-class values were only beautiful, what were you wanting to change in the first place? One minute you claim inequality has left the people ignorant and the next minute you claim you want to do nothing but what the people want. But why should you want to do that which an ignorant people want? What kind of logic is that?

> *MACEY's excitement and confidence animates SIMONE.*

SIMONE: That chair is beautiful because a craftsman exercised his craftsmanship on it. If an unjust society enabled one man to give another man the money to create a beautiful chair, does that make the chair a decadent work of craftsmanship?

MACEY: The trouble is, Simone, they've taught the people to despise the wrong things. That's why their mums and dads ignored their shops.

> *MACEY and SIMONE become collaborators in mocking them.*

SIMONE: You can't come to the people and claim that the things you like are superior to the things they like – that's elitism. And so in their wish not to appear elitist they gave blessings and applause to the most bigoted, the most loud-mouthed, the most reactionary instincts in the people.

> *No response.*

> *SIMONE moves to switch on light over ESTHER's bed.*

But *she* wasn't afraid to be accused of elitism. Esther wasn't obsessed with being responsible only to the twentieth century. Twenty centuries of sensibility, the accumulation of *that* is what she felt responsible to. The past is too rich with human suffering and achievement to be dismissed, she said. In the end there's sweetness in hidden places, someone is always rising up, taking wing, and I want to be there, she said.

No response.

Turning on them.

Esther wouldn't wear cloth caps to make it easy for herself to join the ranks, nor would she walk in rags, nor dress in battledress to prove she shared the worker's cause; nor did she pretend to share his tastes to prove she was the salt of the earth. And I was with her. All the way! Now shoot me for that.

The others seem chastened and mellow, though more touched than convinced.

* * *

MACEY: They've listened, Simone.

After a long silence.

MANFRED: Yes, Simone, we've listened. But our mess is made of other things, like fears, pretensions and disappointments. It's not made of our confusion about who should own eighteenth-century chairs, it's made of – the silly things we've added to the world: easy achievements, ephemeral success. And if you want to thrash the gloom from us then you'd have to give us back youth and the strength not to despise ourselves.

SIMONE: THAT'S NOT GOOD ENOUGH!

She runs to the dead ESTHER and throws back covers.

She wanted to live.

ROLAND: LEAVE HER!

ROLAND snatches the body and hugs it to himself.

SIMONE: You've been wanting to do that all the time, haven't you? But you didn't dare.

> *A strange scene begins; (see note at end of play) at first it seems hysterical, then macabre, but finally must become the natural actions of people trying to find their own way of both showing their love for the dead and trying to overcome their fear of death.*
>
> *Everyone is electrified, uncertain, but sensing SIMONE is about to do something outrageous.*
>
> *SIMONE watches them as though gauging how far she should go and then, cheekily rather than hysterically, raises a dead arm, making it 'wave' at the others.*

She wanted to live.

> *She waits to see what effect it has on them.*
>
> *ROLAND is mesmerized, gripping ESTHER's body fearfully from behind.*
>
> *Now SIMONE makes it appear as though he is embracing her as she forces an arm to reach back and pull down ROLAND's face to kiss the neck.*
>
> *The body seems to have life.*
>
> *Whispering tenderly and reassuringly to ROLAND:*

She wanted to live.

> *How are the others affected?*
>
> *She watches.*
>
> *ROLAND is slowly affected and makes the dead hand blow a kiss. At last a faint smile appears from each one and they shift in embarrassment and shyness, as though caught committing an improper act.*
>
> *SIMONE realizes she's broken through.*

She did! She wanted to live.

Encouraged, she pushes them further by bringing 'Esther's chair' to centre of room, and facing it towards the portrait of Lenin.

> *ROLAND understands and carries the dead ESTHER to sit in the chair.*
>
> *MANFRED also understands and reaches for a cushion to prop up her head.*
>
> *The understanding spreads as TESSA picks up a stool to lay for her feet.*
>
> *MANFRED bends ESTHER's hand into a clenched-fist salute.*
>
> *The arm holds aloft for a short while then slowly falls telling us that the revolutionary zeal the clenched fist once represented, has failed.*
>
> *CRISPIN finds a book to place in her hands. Thus seated, the others are forced to accept the presence of the dead among them. Slowly they relax and one by one kiss her cheek, then –*
>
> *MANFRED returns to his model.*
>
> *TESSA and CRISPIN go to the bed to fold the blankets.*
>
> *ROLAND sits by ESTHER as though guarding her.*
>
> *SIMONE clears away coffee cups and dirty ashtrays.*
>
> *MACEY watches them a while, reaches for his jacket, half leaves, turns to smile at ROLAND, returns to kiss ESTHER, leaves –*
>
> *a slow, slow fading away.*
>
> *The End.*

Special Note:

Because the last minutes of the play may seem bizarre or far-fetched let me report that the idea of handling the dead body of ESTHER came from a Romanian ritual I was told about in that country where, to help recovering from the grief of losing a beloved one, the family was encouraged to hold the dead body under the arm pits and jump with it in a kind of macabre dance. It was thought that the comicality of such a dance would achieve laughter and thus detract from the pain of loss.

BLUEY

a play in one act and three parts

Characters

A play for fifteen characters to be performed by eight actors.

Author's Note

This is a play about suppressed guilt.

A retired judge, Hilary Hawkins, is journeying through the past to discover what happened then to give him a nervous breakdown now.

The play's convention calls for actors to play many roles. They are, apart from his wife, characters from his past who stand by in their settings watching him make his painful journey, waiting to be called upon to play their part in his life and help him understand.

The convention allows for HILARY to remain in his study while the other characters speak to him from their setting.

Once a setting is established in the text it will not be repeatedly identified except where it helps the reader.

It's important for the tension of the piece that this structure be followed.

It will also enable the play to unfold without pause and with that inexorability the story calls for.

Main Roles

1 HILARY HAWKINS
a High Court Judge, aged about fifty-eight

2 SOPHIE
his wife, aged about fifty-five

3 MRS HAWKINS
his mother, aged about seventy-eight

4 RON KIMBLE
a Cockney plumber, young at twenty-five, old at sixty-five

Secondary Roles

5 MARTIN SEYMOUR SCOTT
wine salesman, aged thirty-two

6 STRIVEN
a scrap-metal merchant, aged forty-three

5 YOUNG HILARY
carpenter's mate, aged about eighteen

7 AUDREY
his girlfriend, young at fifteen, older at forty

6 TOM VINTERS
a Cockney carpenter, young at twenty, old at sixty

3 KATIE
Jewish delicatessen shopkeeper, about sixty

Minor Roles

6 COUNSEL FOR THE PLAINTIFF

RADIO ANNOUNCER

8 FRIEND OF HILARY'S
stockbroker, aged fifty

8 RORY KELLY
Belfast Irish plumber's mate, about eighteen

7 MRS MONTGOMERY
a housewife, about thirty-five

3 MRS MITCHUM
a housewife, about forty-five

Two different actors have to play HILARY as young and old. But I leave it to the discretion of the director whether two actors are needed to play the young and old other characters of RON KIMBLE, AUDREY and TOM VINTERS. My guess is that it would be less confusing and more of a challenge for the actors if one played both ages.

Important

Sound plays a central role and should be orchestrated
with great attention to detail.

Part One – Remembering

Darkness.

Out of it a voice cries long, drawn out 'Below – ow – ow – ow.'

A second's pause, then – a thud followed immediately by a cry of pain.

Silence.

Sound of rain, wind, scratching of a pen on paper.

HILARY'S VOICE: I sit here, as I have sat over the years, listening to the rain, wondering will it ever stop.

Lights up.

HILARY'S STUDY

JUDGE HILARY HAWKINS alone in his country cottage, writing his diary.

Around, in their various settings, are the characters from his past and present life who are watching and waiting to be called upon to help him understand that which troubles him.

HILARY: *(Writing.)* Though it could happen in no better place high in these Black Mountains of Wales where, I remember an old aunt warning, it always rains.

Pen down. Looks around.

You bought it, though, didn't you, Hilary? Bid two thousand five hundred against a woman who bid two thousand, rain or no rain. Worth fifty times that now.

Looks closely at a dilapidated armchair.

Auction furniture! Change it! Children gone – too many memories.

Returns to diary. Writes.

Needed to retreat here to work. Sift the lies from the truth. Consider judgements.

Pen down.

All those sad men and women who passed through your court, what a great mess they'd made of their lives. You couldn't ever pass judgement on anybody again, could you?

Voice crying 'Below – ow – ow – ow'.

The thud.

The cry of pain.

They seem to be sounds within, briefly puzzling him.

I don't understand. 'Below'? 'Below?' And you thought you had recovered, didn't you, Hilary? Poor Sophie, this diary worries her.

HAWKIN'S LONDON HOME – THE KITCHEN

SOPHIE HAWKINS talks to HILARY who, the convention allows, remains in his Welsh study.

SOPHIE: It's like being in competition with another woman. You tell her things you don't tell me. Makes me feel inadequate. What's she got that I haven't?

HILARY: 'She' has the virtue of never being confused by my contradictions. Nor can 'she' answer back. No! I don't mean that. A diary can't *condemn* you. No! *Judge* you. No! *Pity* you.

Pause.

Am I recovered? Why this torment then, this sense of something unfinished?

Pause.

I remember, when I first came here I'd sleep with a heavy stick beside me. Nervous. Nervous about everything. Even crossing the courtyard in the dark from the study to the main house. Had a madman entered while I'd been at work? Don't be stupid – I'd talk aloud to myself – there's no one. Just you, the night, the hills – isolation! No one!

But – isolation, howling winds, night – stirs the imagination.

Sound swells of howling wind and rain.

Rain! Oh the injustice of days without sun. I long for a clear day, a starry night, some warmth for my old bones.

Sorry, Sophie. I suppose it *is* insulting to talk to a diary rather than a wife.

SOPHIE: I'm not insulted, Hilary, I'm worried. I know you need privacy but it's not good to be alone. Solitude doesn't incline a man to be fair to himself. You'll get lonely, then self-contempt will creep in, then recrimination, then self-pity. I warn you, you'll discover sins you didn't know you had. They'll proliferate like a plague after the fall.

HILARY: 'A plague after the fall'. You'd have made a better counsel than me, Sophie. I'll never understand why you gave it up. The money was there – au pairs, nannies, anything you wanted.

SOPHIE: Guilt! I couldn't reconcile the two lives – law and domesticity. Besides, if I must be honest, I prefer domestic life. Gave me more freedom to do what I liked rather than what I *had* to do to prove I was free.

HILARY: Clever wife!

Returns to diary. Writes.

Why do I sit here, as I have sat over the years, listening to the rain. What do I imagine I am doing?

Stops writing.

It's as though I'm waiting for something. What, Hilary, what 'something'? Something to assemble. Like the film of a smashed vase run backwards. Ah! You mean *re*-assemble. But what?

> *Voice crying 'Below – ow – ow – ow'*
>
> *The thud.*
>
> *The cry of pain.*

'Below'. What an absurd word. Why do I keep hearing it? Wherever I go – a stroll, a shop, a dinner party: 'below, below, below!' A conspiracy to unnerve me. What am I being told? And by a boring preposition! Not even a conceptual word! Not even an adjective. 'Beware' – I'd have felt something. 'Death' – I might have understood. Or liar, bigot, blind, scream, fear, money, silence! A word that warned, echoed with portent, rang resonant – but 'below'?

Here I sit writing my diary in this study with damp walls, listening to the rain, trying to remember – when did I first hear the word.

COURTROOM

> *COUNSEL FOR THE PLAINTIFF addresses HILARY, 'the judge in court', who, even though in his house, listens.*

COUNSEL: And so, my Lord, we have a case before us precisely for which the law was designed. We have heard witness after witness brought by Mr Scott's defence counsel to describe my client, James Striven, as being what the world might regard as an unpleasant personality – mean, avaricious, morbid, sordidly pursuing pornography as a pastime – as though to be unloveable is a crime, or more to the point is *justification* for a crime. But to be unloveable – fortunately for many of us – is not a crime. A man may be as socially unacceptable as he please yet must he enjoy equal protection under the law as those who may not wish, socially, to accept him.

My client's property and privacy were invaded and his character besmirched, and all for the Galahad cock-and-bull inventions of Mr Scott. We could be, but we are not, demanding damages for deformation – that would be to give credence to Scott's fantastic allegations. But the law of property is sacrosanct and my client's claim for damages for trespass must be pressed. The sanctity of law must be upheld not only if the strong trespass upon the weak from on high but also, difficult though it may be to contemplate, when the weak clamber up and trespass upon the strong from below.

> *The word 'below' is repeated and echoed like a recurrent tune in the head.*
>
> *VOICE OF RADIO ANNOUNCER.*
>
> *Everyone is listening.*

RADIO ANNOUNCER: And now for financial report. The Financial Times share index has dropped from yesterday's spectacular rise to below…

> *The word 'below' is repeated and echoed like a recurrent tune in the head.*
>
> *SOPHIE on the phone to HILARY.*

SOPHIE: But Hilary, my darling, what does it matter if you're only using the study. You have to go back into the house at nights and I don't want you going back into a cold house. What if you want to read a novel in bed.

HILARY: Buy me an electric blanket.

SOPHIE: Don't be stingy. Keep the heating on during the day.

HILARY: I *do* keep it on during the day, it's just that I put the thermostat down to fifty degrees. We must save oil, Sophie, it's expensive.

SOPHIE: Fine. Save it! But promise me you'll keep the thermostat at fifty degrees and not below…

> *The word 'below' is repeated and echoed like a recurrent tune in the head but this time ends as a shout from on high.*
>
> *The thud.*
>
> *The cry of pain.*

HILARY'S STUDY

HILARY: They were not good years for me. Not good at all. Confused judgement followed judgement ill-considered, and each one turned over on appeal. How on earth did I ever become a judge? What powers had I once revealed that commanded respect and now seem to be receding. No! Draining! No! Weakening!

I have this memory. My study in London, a room where I burnt the midnight oil wrestling with conflicting evidence to arrive at a judgement; a room where I'd entertained friends and colleagues, made love. I stood there. In the middle of that room. Stood there looking at the shelf of books and records, the prints on the wall, the hand picked furniture, the objects which I'd long forgotten had come from whom for what reason. And I thought: what has any of this to do with me? I'm a stranger in this room. Why am I lingering? And because I could see no setting in which I belonged, no alternative life, I experienced the most extraordinary sense of levitation. No! Floating! No! Disembodiment! No! Discontinuity! No! No! The word should be – disorientation. But it's not. Not quite. Not precise. Displacement! Better. I was displaced from the life I had so painstakingly assembled. I was adrift. Of no fixed address. Bereft. Ah! 'Bereft'. A wealth of a word, that one. Bereft. And afraid.

> *Swell the sound of rain.*

Not good years at all. I lost my nerve, my courage, my appetite for things.

COURTROOM

COUNSEL FOR PLAINTIFF and SCOTT

COUNSEL: Please give the court your name and age and nature of employment.

SCOTT: My name is Martin Seymour Scott, I'm aged thirty-two, and I work in Harrods selling wine.

COUNSEL: Now, will you tell my Lord, in your own words, exactly what happened that drew you into Mister Striven's house.

SCOTT: I suppose it began from the first day Striven and his wife moved in next door. He was an angry man, vicious. He seemed never to shave or wash and no one dared answer him back because he had the look of someone who wouldn't think twice about laying hands on you. And his voice was like…like…like a slow knife. I remember he made a fire in the garden. The very first week. A huge fire, which stank. God knows what he was burning, but it stank and made black smoke which blocked out the sun and dropped soot and ashes over all our houses. Every week I had to clean my window ledges, and I watched his flowers die, his grass grow, and his shrubs strangle one another, and I couldn't understand any of it. They weren't poor. He was a wealthy scrap merchant, wasn't he? Employed people.

> *Pause.*

And in the night there was the screaming of his wife.

One day I took the afternoon off to comeback early and speak with her. She invited me in. It was a neat house, sir, clean, and well stocked. But I could see he beat her. What do you do in a situation like that? It's not easy to report neighbours to the police, and it's not easy to live near suffering and remain quiet. Especially for an Englishman. No Englishman likes interfering in other people's lives. But in the end I couldn't bear it. One evening I knocked on the door in the middle of his rantings and asked him to stop it and leave his wife alone. And that voice, that slow knife, it cut back at me.

A STREET FRONT DOOR

STRIVEN to SCOTT.

STRIVEN: Oh, and what shall we do about it? Shall we strike me violently? Shall Sir Galahad apprehend me, report me? Who to? What for? It would give me great pleasure to smash your face into my mantlepiece and stick your head down my lavatory pan, Mister Scott. But that would only land me in deep with the law and give you satisfaction.

Instead, you listen to me and you listen very hard. There's a fence around this house, and everything in it belongs to me. The air, the space, the smells, the dirt bins, every brick, windowsill, drain and all the living creatures within it. Even the overgrown grass I know you hate because I see you mow your lawn like clockwork – mine! To do with as I please. Which no one inside or outside the law can touch or tell me how to manage. My possessions! Belonging to me! Mine!

Now, I have given you five minutes inside these fences. *I've* been generous and *you've* been lucky. You've got thirty seconds to get out or I will do things no law court could deny me the right to do. Fuck off from my territory. And don't forget it *is* my territory. Don't forget …

> *The phrase 'don't forget' is repeated and echoed like a recurrent tune in the head.*

HILARY: Poor Scott! He left shaking. Felt as though he'd come face to face with the devil. It made him sick. He had to stay away from work.

SOPHIE: But why did he go back to the man's house?

HILARY: He heard this terrible howling.

THE STRIVEN'S CELLAR

STRIVEN's wife, half-naked, in chains. Beaten. She's howling.

HILARY: Striven was at his scrap yard. Scott found a window ajar, got in that way.

> *SCOTT confronts the chained woman.*

> *He falters at the sight. When recovered sufficiently he attempts to unchain her.*

MRS STRIVEN: Don't! I beg you! Leave me!

SCOTT: Leave you?

MRS STRIVEN: I'm alright.

SCOTT: Like this?

MRS STRIVEN: Go.

SCOTT: Like *this*?

MRS STRIVEN: Yes. Like this. He'll be back soon and he's got to find me like this.

SCOTT: *Got* to? Like this? Like this? Oh, Jesus Christ, like *this*?

MRS STRIVEN: Exactly. Nothing changed. If I even attempt to release myself and he sees the signs he beats me more.

SCOTT: Why don't you…how can you…

MRS STRIVEN: I'm used to it. It's pain but it's bearable.

SCOTT: What does he think… I mean…

MRS STRIVEN: Go!

SCOTT: This is monstrous. This is absolutely unbelievably monstrous.

MRS STRIVEN: Go!

SCOTT: It mustn't be.

MRS STRIVEN: Go. I beg you!

SCOTT: This is criminal.

MRS STRIVEN: Go! Go!

SCOTT: How can I go and leave this…this…this…

MRS STRIVEN: Go and say nothing to anyone. Not a soul. If you care for my safety you must promise not to say a word.

SCOTT: I can't…

MRS STRIVEN: Promise!

SCOTT: I…

MRS STRIVEN: Promise!

SCOTT: It's not possible… It's not…

MRS STRIVEN: *(With sudden total control.)* If you do not go immediately I will scream until someone comes and I will accuse you of doing this thing to me.

SCOTT: You…you will…you will *what?*

MRS STRIVEN: Go!

SCOTT: This is beyond anything I…

MRS STRIVEN: And it will always be beyond anything you understand. Now go! Go! Go!

> *SCOTT's words choke in his throat. He seems on the verge of fainting, or hysteria as he retreats before this demonic woman.*

Go! Go! And say nothing to anyone. Remember you promised. Don't forget you promised. You promised. Don't forget, don't forget, don't forget…

*The phrase 'don't forget' is repeated and echoed like
a recurrent tune in the head.*

HILARY: At which point he conceived his quixotic plan to
liberate her and take her to a little cottage he imagined
he could buy in the country, though with what I couldn't
ascertain.

SOPHIE: Poor fool.

HILARY: Poor fool indeed. His cunning neighbour could see
he had an idiot next door. Scott waited till he judged it
the right moment to enter Striven's house and release the
chained slave but –

SOPHIE: – there was no chained slave.

HILARY: Just Striven, and a neat, seemingly bewildered wife.
They called the police, Scott told his story, the police
investigated the cellar and –

SOPHIE: – and found nothing.

HILARY: It was obvious to all of us in court that Striven was
lying and Scott was telling the truth. But the law had to
support the liar because, even had such a torture chamber
existed and the lie been discovered, the lie was irrelevant.
Striven had turned from the sadistic satisfactions of wife-
beating to the thrill of trapping his poor neighbour into
trespass for which he now claimed damages.

SOPHIE: And you could do nothing?

HILARY: I was powerless.

COURTROOM

SCOTT, STRIVEN and an immaculate MRS STRIVEN.

MRS STRIVEN: I can't begin to imagine where Mister Scott
got his disgusting fantasies from. It makes me feel unclean
just to have listened to him. I knew many men before
my husband and there was not one of them, not one

who measured up to his kindness. You've seen, sir, all
the letters of thank-you received from the charities to
which my husband has donated not – I might tell you
– inconsiderable sums. I've even attempted to curb his
generosity, but it's no use. Once my husband's heart is
touched it is touched very deeply, I can assure you.

STRIVEN: He's not liked me from the day I first moved in next
to him. Kept complaining I blocked out his sunlight.

Shouting at SCOTT.

I've never once crossed your threshold to do you a bad
turn, Scott, have I? Have I?

HILARY: Mister Striven…

STRIVEN: You interfering scheming bastard!

HILARY: Mister Striven control yourself in court.

STRIVEN: *(Ignoring him.)* You wanted to get me but I've got
you.

HILARY: Mister Striven I …

STRIVEN: I told you it was my territory. I warned you.

HILARY: Mister Striven, if you don't desist you will be in
contempt of court and I may have to –

STRIVEN: *(Forging ahead.)* 'Don't forget' I told you. 'My
territory' I said, '*my* territory. Don't forget!' I said 'don't
forget! don't forget…'

*The phrase 'don't forget' is repeated and echoed like
a recurrent tune in the head.*

HILARY: That phrase 'don't forget'. A second one knocking at
my memory. 'Below' and now 'don't forget', persistent, like
a melody clamouring to be recognised. Everyone seemed
to use the words. My clerk kept telling me not to forget
things. 'Don't forget, don't forget, don't forget – below!' I
knew it referred to something familiar, but what? What?

Striven, that venomous dealer in discarded metals, he'd
stirred some recess in my mind. I'd never met a man
in whose nature was concentrated so much ugliness.
No! Bestiality! No! Cruelty! No! Malevolence! His wife
had insisted upon his kindness but for me he was a bleak
landscape, his charity like bribes to heaven's gatekeepers.
Winter promises spring but *his* nature was relentlessly
dark, a frozen pity promising only cruelty. He offended
me, sapped my will, tore at my spirit, hit me at my darkest
suspicions. I couldn't let the law win him justice, nor could I
bring myself to distort the law which was in his favour. The
good man was wrong, the evil one right. It was a conflict I
could neither support nor resolve. Inevitable that I'd crack.
And I did. Crumbled. Like an obsolete steeple. Crumbled
and cracked. And through the crumbles and cracks crept all
the shames of my past. One by shameful one.

MRS HAWKIN'S FLAT

*HILARY's mother has just been shopping. She has
returned to find HILARY waiting for her.*

MRS HAWKINS: Fee fi fo fum I smell the tobacco of my long
lost son.

HILARY: Not 'long lost', just busy, mother. Here, let me bring
those carriers in for you.

MRS HAWKINS: Weighed down by the criminal world, are
you?

HILARY: They don't have to be criminals to depress me. Good
God! You live alone – and all this shopping?

MRS HAWKINS: I shop once every two weeks for the essentials.

HILARY: I'll unpack them.

MRS HAWKINS: You always loved unpacking the shopping.
Nice orderly mind you had.

HILARY: Not so orderly these days.

MRS HAWKINS: Oh?

HILARY: There's this case I've been working through. A man called Striven. Outwardly generous, respectable but –

MRS HAWKINS: But what?

HILARY: I sense evil in him as I've sensed it in no one before, and I find it profoundly disturbing. As though –

MRS HAWKINS: As though?

HILARY: I don't know. He tires me. I musn't bring the court home. Forget it.

MRS HAWKINS: Guess who I saw?

HILARY: The Ghost of Time Past?

MRS HAWKINS: Almost. Little Audrey.

HILARY: Audrey?

MRS HAWKINS: Remember? And little Audrey laughed and laughed…

YOUNG HILARY'S HOME

His parent's are out. Energetic section of Rimsky-Korsakov's 'Scheherazade'.

YOUNG HILARY and his girlfriend, AUDREY. Both are naked. She's riding him.

Spring awakenings!

AUDREY: *(Giggling and seductive.)* And little Audrey laughed and laughed and laughed. Stand, Hilary, come, be a good boy and stand for Audrey.

YOUNG HILARY: Oh Christ, Audrey, but you're incredible. You're so open and shameless and happy about it.

AUDREY: Why not? It's all natural. You enjoy it, I enjoy it, they enjoy it. I only wish we could do it more often. But you and your law studies! You're such an egghead, so difficult to get hold of.

YOUNG HILARY: What about these muscles, Audrey, all that holiday work on building sites – feel.

AUDREY: Stupid boy! Imagining I care about muscles. It's who you are not what you feel like. What do I care about your stupid muscles and your labouring on building sites. Oh, Hilary, aren't you a *little* in love with me?

YOUNG HILARY: I think you're unique, isn't that enough?

AUDREY: I'm in love with you, Hilary. It can't be enough.

YOUNG HILARY: Be my mistress.

AUDREY: I don't want to be your short-term mistress, I want to be your forever-sweetheart-with-a-ring-on-my-finger. Two rings, in fact.

Passion intensifies.

YOUNG HILARY: Oh Christ, Audrey. God in heaven! What are you doing to me?

AUDREY: I've got all sorts of lovely things in store for you if you behave yourself.

YOUNG HILARY: Don't you think you ought to behave *your*self?

AUDREY: Lie still.

YOUNG HILARY: How can I lie still when you're exciting me so?

As she rides she sings over 'Scheherazade'.

AUDREY: *My uncle he was a Spanish captain*
Went to sea a month ago
First he kissed me then he left me
Bade me always answer 'no'.
Oh, no John, no John, no John, no!

YOUNG HILARY: Ahhhhhhh! *(Orgasm.)* I want to cry. No! Shout! No! Dance! No! – I don't know what I want to do.

AUDREY: Aren't you a *little* bit in love with me? A little? Just a little, little, leeetle?

MRS HAWKIN'S FLAT

HILARY: We were all a little bit in love with her. Initiated us.

MRS HAWKINS: But she wasn't more than fifteen!

HILARY: And we were all older and very, very lusty.

MRS HAWKINS: You should have known better, then.

HILARY: It was her pleasure to pleasure us.

MRS HAWKINS: I don't want to hear about it.

HILARY: Nothing crude. Nothing smutty. Sweet. She was sweet and good-natured. Consoling when we despaired, reprimanding when we succumbed to self-pity. The first sunny person I ever knew.

MRS HAWKINS: And she's still sunny. Still got that smile. Lights up the street – cheeky, mischievous.

HILARY: She'd have been happy to wive us all, with a dozen rings on her fingers and a dozen more on her toes.

MRS HAWKINS: She asked after you. Says she follows all your cases in the press. Says there's something she wants to talk to you about.

AUDREY ON HER PHONE

But we hear it as though at the other end of the receiver.

AUDREY: No, don't panic, Hilary. I'm not going to ask you for a hand-out now that you've been made a judge. I bet you get a lot of that – strangers or old school chums asking for hand-outs, thinking you must be rich. Not Audrey.

Wouldn't even if I needed it. But I'll come to the point, mustn't waste your time listening to my nonsense. On the other hand – I'm going to contradict myself now – on the other hand I *would* like you to give a little time up for me. You see – I'm not well. No, don't say anything! Just listen a little. Doctors don't know what's wrong, they never do, do they? And I'm feeling a little low. I'd perfectly understand if you couldn't. Honestly I would. But every so often, when I go shopping in Finsbury Park, I see your Mother, and she tells me about you and so I've got this urge, for old time's sake, just to natter, go over the past, gossip a bit. Would you? I've got no right to ask, really. We drifted apart. I know that. And it's always difficult meeting old friends. Never know what you'll find. But would you? Come and see me? I'm a bit fatter, not as pretty as I was, and I don't laugh so much these days.

MRS HAWKIN'S FLAT

HILARY is leaving and will conduct his telephone conversation with AUDREY from the London house.

MRS HAWKINS: The doctors knew alright. Cancer! I met her in Finsbury Park out shopping, took one look at her and knew. Cancer! Sure as eggs is eggs.

HILARY: I told her I'd ring to make a date as soon as the case was over.

MRS HAWKINS: See her, Hilary. I think you should. She always asks about you, and she was a good friend. Even *I* liked her, and I didn't like many of your friends.

TELEPHONE CONVERSATION

Sound of phone ringing. AUDREY picks it up.

AUDREY: Hello, Mountview 3105.

HILARY: Audrey?

AUDREY: Speaking.

HILARY: It's Hilary.

AUDREY: Hilary!

HILARY: I'm ringing to make that date.

AUDREY: Oh, no! I'm all embarrassed now. Don't know what to say.

HILARY: I want to know what this nonsense is about being ill.

AUDREY: I wish it was nonsense. I prefer talking nonsense. Never did like being serious. Remember?

HILARY: I remember a lot of things, Audrey.

AUDREY: Uh-uh! Naughty! No naughty reminiscences.

HILARY: I thought that's what you *wanted* to do – reminisce.

AUDREY: There's reminisce and reminisce.

HILARY: How are you?

AUDREY: What can I tell you? I'm not a well person.

HILARY: I'm coming to see you.

AUDREY: You're a good boy, Hilary.

HILARY: No longer a boy, Audrey, I've got three young teenagers.

AUDREY: Oh, how I'd love to see them.

HILARY: You will, you will. You'll come with your husband to dinner.

AUDREY: You won't like my husband, Hilary. He's not your sort. A bit rough, Jack. Not bad at heart but – rough. Impatient with the world. Full of opinions but no thought. What *you* would call a reactionary.

HILARY: Will he approve of me coming to see you?

AUDREY: Come when he's at work. What the eye doesn't see…

Phones down.

HILARY moves sadly to –

HILARY'S STUDY

AUDREY picks up the phone again. Again we hear it through the receiver. HILARY is listening as though remembering.

AUDREY: I'm sorry, Hilary. I must cancel our date. I'm too ill. Look really awful. I don't want you to see me looking awful. Vain of me I know, at my age, but that's how it is. Wait a little, will you? Till I'm better? I'll be better soon, and I *would* like to see you, honest, it's been so long. What have we all done with the time, eh? The doctors say this will pass. Ring me in a couple of weeks, will you? Please? *You* ring *me*, that way I'll know it's not me nagging but you wanting. Promise? Two weeks time. The doctors have this new drug…

Swell sound of rain, of wind.

HILARY: I didn't ring. Made no contact at all. She'd been so pretty, such a sweet and generous soul, I just couldn't face her dying. That bloated skin hairy from drugs? I'd have wept. She'd have seen her dying in my eyes. Wasn't strong enough for the pain of that. Nor the pain of anything. Something had snapped in me. Disaster headlines in the press and I'd move on. The sight of starving children on television, I'd weep. If I saw rudeness in my children or insensitivity I'd rage. That was my cracked and crumbling state. I was incapable of giving comfort. Just couldn't go. And I was so ashamed. Audrey would have come to *my* death bed. With all her lack of sophistication, her absence of what's called 'good taste' she would have found the right tone of voice, pitched her sunniness at the right angle. Not too high, not too bright, not too hot – but a cool summer's evening full of drunk bees and trivia.

HILARY's remembering what his mother said.

MRS HAWKINS: It was good you didn't go, son. You'd have been very upset. It's better this way. You'll remember her as she was. I think she really wanted that, that's why she cancelled your first date. She wanted to see you but she didn't want you to see her. She'd have gone on cancelling dates for ever.

HILARY is writing and weeping.

HILARY: Forgive me, Audrey. I hope you had around you those you loved. I hope you were cared for and cherished. Forgive me. You were never forgotten.

Pen down.

Oh Christ, Audrey, you wouldn't approve of these tears, would you?

I sit here, as I've sat over the years, listening to the rain, remembering these things. Not good years for me. Cracked and crumbling years, and through the crumbles and cracks have crept out all the shames of my past. One by shameful one.

Sound of wind and rain swells.

LONDON KITCHEN

HILARY is reading a letter.

HILARY: God help me, Sophie. Another letter from the past.

SOPHIE: Anyone you remember? Liked?

HILARY: *(Reading.)* '*Dear comrade of long ago. Before you look at the signature at the end of the letter please can I ask you not to.*'

SOPHIE: Sounds intriguing.

HILARY: I hate guessing games.

SOPHIE: Might be an old girlfriend.

HILARY: Girlfriends don't call one 'comrade'.

SOPHIE: Don't snap at me, darling.

HILARY: I'm too busy for guessing games. I have to face this
man Striven every day in court and he's the most deeply
unpleasant and distressing personality I've ever had to
cope with.

SOPHIE: Sometimes voices from the past can be soothing.
Read it.

HILARY: *'Dear comrade of long ago. Before you look at the
signature...*

FRIEND takes over.

FRIEND: Before you look at the signature at the end of the
letter please can I ask you not to. It is important that I try
to remind you of the things that we experienced together
and of course perhaps also finding out what things you
remember me by.

Let me give you clues. It was the days of conscription. I
was clever and spoilt, destined to become an officer; you
were struggling against the fates, the Finsbury Park Fates as
your mother once sardonically described them.

We square-bashed together, me hating it, you being
philosophical. It was you got me through those eight
absurd weeks of basic training. Made me feel very humble.
I thought we'd never meet again. But coincidence!
Coincidence! We did! Studied law together. Are you
remembering me yet?

Law was too demanding for my kind of butterfly brilliance.
Only stuck it for two years.

You must remember me by now. Or perhaps I'm very
forgettable. Why do I write? I don't know, really. Yes, I
do! You see, I was fifty, four months ago. My children are
grown up and gone away and I'm left with those Sundays
in which husbands face boring wives who find their
husbands boring. But I'm not writing out of boredom.

Let me be blunt. I'm frightened. I've lost that still centre.
I wake up not understanding where I am or what I'm
supposed to be doing. With all my cleverness I've placed
myself among people who neither touch me nor make
sense. I don't see the point of their existence, not in
relationship to me anyway. And my memory of you is of
a being with a very still centre. All things had their place
when you were around. And so I wondered, could we
meet, have a drink together, share a meal.

I know it's a long time. But please would you bear it, for
old time's sake? Best wishes, your friend of long ago. PS.
Do you ever get the feeling you want to climb a roof and
shout out? I don't know what, but something. Just simply
to – shout out.

> *The phrase 'shout out' is repeated and echoed like a*
> *recurrent tune in the head.*

SOPHIE: And do you remember him?

HILARY: Indeed I do. Even with affection. He was the first
person from the 'upper classes' I'd ever encountered. And
sunny. Like Audrey.

SOPHIE: Who laughed and laughed.

HILARY: And he was clever with it. Unlike me. I had to force
my brain to function. We used to walk a lot together and
he'd tease me for working so hard.

SOPHIE: Why don't you meet up with him?

HILARY: Worried. He seems afflicted with darkness. Like a
virus. Contagious.

SOPHIE: That's not like you, Hilary.

HILARY: Don't I have dark viruses of my own to wrestle with?

SOPHIE: Does one 'wrestle' with a virus?

HILARY: No! Stem! No! Eradicate! No! Combat!

SOPHIE: Better! You *combat* viruses.

HILARY: Or we'd meet, he'd get maudlin, drunk, ask my opinions on all the big issues of the world, wait for wise judgements, have unbearable expectations.

SOPHIE: Well you have got opinions. And you *are* full of wise judgements.

HILARY: You think *that* because you love me. 'Shout from the rooftop'. I understand what he means but I couldn't join him there. I'd open my mouth and no sound would come out.

SOPHIE: Those hills, that isolation...

MRS HAWKIN'S FLAT

MRS HAWKINS is ill, sits in an armchair with blanket over her.

HILARY appears.

MRS HAWKINS: I knew you'd come. I heard the telephone but just couldn't reach it so I knew you'd come.

HILARY: What is it?

MRS HAWKINS: I'm ill, that's what it is.

HILARY: Why didn't you phone back?

MRS HAWKINS: I couldn't move, that's why.

HILARY: You should be living with us.

MRS HAWKINS: Mothers can't live with daughters-in-law. It's not fair to either of them. Especially strong personalities like Sophie and I.

HILARY: Sophie and me.

MRS HAWKINS: Sophie and me. I love it when you correct my grammar.

HILARY: That's the only reason I do it, *because* you love it.

MRS HAWKINS: Reminds me I've got an educated son.

HILARY: What do I care how you speak.

MRS HAWKINS: Oh you should, Hilary, you should. To have a mum you're proud of? Important.

HILARY: Live nearer, I'll care.

MRS HAWKINS: Not possible.

HILARY: Loneliness is a killer.

MRS HAWKINS: Oh, it's not so bad. It's bad, but it's not *so* bad. I shop, I read my paper, clean a bit each day, keep an eye on my neighbours. I even go to the cinema now and then, riding around on the top of buses. Lovely! Everything's cheap for old age pensioners, you know.

HILARY: The old shouldn't be left alone.

MRS HAWKINS: Old is old and there it is.

HILARY: A house and children need grandparents.

MRS HAWKINS: I like sleeping late, I like listening to my favourite radio programme, I like windows open.

HILARY: The old, the young, Sophie and I in the middle.

MRS HAWKINS: Sophie and me!

HILARY: Sophie and me!

MRS HAWKINS: *I'd* be in the middle, silly boy. Where's your head? Clients going to law need a hard head. Forget me and build your practice.

HILARY: My practice is big enough.

MRS HAWKINS: It can never be big enough. Forget me, build your practice and make your head harder.

HILARY: You're not short, are you?

MRS HAWKINS: Keep your money, Hilary.

HILARY: You wouldn't deny me *that* pleasure, would you?

MRS HAWKINS: You have a bank overdraft, a wife who doesn't understand how money works, and children who don't *care* how money works. Forget me, build your practice, make your head harder. I have sufficient.

HILARY: If we found the money to buy a flat nearer us, would you move?

MRS HAWKINS: You're a real nag, Hilary.

HILARY: Would you?

MRS HAWKINS: I've moved enough! I'm tired of getting used to new things.

HILARY: You'd be able to pop in and out.

MRS HAWKINS: And get on Sophie's nerves.

HILARY: She's very fond of you.

MRS HAWKINS: So she should be. I'm a very nice person. I've kept my distance.

HILARY: Is that what being a very nice person is?

MRS HAWKINS: It helps, Hilary, it helps.

HILARY: You could have died!

MRS HAWKINS: So? Bad thing! Old is old! What can you do? Besides, I never wanted to grow into decrepitry.

HILARY: Decrepitude.

MRS HAWKINS: See! A lower middle-class life shows through. Decrepitude. I always hoped that when it was time to go I'd be tired and *want* to go. Well, I'm getting tired, my child.

HILARY: No longer 'child', mother.

MRS HAWKINS: You'll be a child till I'm dead. And when I'm dead you'll be nobody's child.

HILARY: I'll get my secretary to contact local estate agents. We'll start looking at once. I'll call the bank.

MRS HAWKINS: Old is old.

HILARY: Somehow or other we'll have you as near as dammit.

MRS HAWKINS: Old is old and that's it. That's it and there it is.

HILARY: And next time call for a neighbour.

MRS HAWKINS: Silly boy! When I'm ill I'm too weak even to shout out.

> *The phrase 'shout out' is repeated and echoed like a recurrent tune in the head.*

HILARY'S STUDY

HILARY: But it never happened. Oh, we looked at a dozen flats but none of them were good enough. *And* she resisted, and Sophie *was* reluctant, and work *was* pressing, and the money never really looked as if it was there, and so she died one day, a long way from us, and I was not there to comfort her. And she was right – suddenly I was no one's son anymore.

So – I sit here as I've sat over the years, listening to the rain, remembering these things, hearing voices…

> *Sound of rain and wind swells.*
>
> *Over it – voices.*

STRIVEN: I don't want you to do me the favour of loving me, Mister Scott. I'm unloveable, and very pleased to be that way. Imagine! All that *you* love and admire I hate and despise: the beautiful, the clever! Playful children, crying babies! Music, lovers, music lovers, spring, animals, God believers, Christ followers, good-cause-collectors-at-the-door! Contempt for them all! Except one – 'Help The Aged'. The old and forgotten are the ones I care about. For the rest – weepers and whiners. The bleeding hearts of the world who imagine they know what's wrong with my life. But I have a fence round my house and everything within that fence is mine. Untouchable! Don't you forget that, ever, don't you forget, don't forget…

> *The phrase 'don't forget' is repeated and echoed like a recurrent tune in the head.*

> *Over it – another voice.*

SCOTT: He had the look of someone who wouldn't think twice about laying hands on you… And his voice was like a slow knife… They weren't poor… He was a wealthy scrap-metal merchant, wasn't he…?

> *The words 'scrap-metal merchant' are repeated and echoed like a recurrent tune in the head.*

> *HILARY struggles to piece the jigsaw together.*

HILARY: My clerk kept telling me not to forget things. 'Don't forget! Don't forget! Don't forget!' I knew it referred to something familiar but what? *What?* And then there was the personality of Striven himself. That venomous dealer in discarded metal…

> *The words 'discarded metals' are repeated and echoed like a recurrent tune in the head.*

> *Over them is blended the word 'below' – repeated and echoed. 'Below – ow – ow – ow' – a shout from on high.*

> *The thud.*

> *The cry of pain.*

> *The sound of swelling rain and wind.*

> *Over it –*

HILARY: I had turned my back on a dying friend, I had remained silent before the plea of an erstwhile chum, I had left my mother to live and die alone. Terrible! Terrible! Terrible! And I sit here as I've sat over the years, remembering and listening to those words like a tumour in the head, 'below…don't forget…shout out…' and I watch the times move, stupefied by civil wars and revenge, assassinations and rhetoric, nationalism and famine, and I know he's touched me, that man, Striven, touched me. No! Scarred me. No! Gnawed at me. Yes! Gnawed at me like a rat deep into my darkest suspicions. Terrible! Terrible! Terrible! And I envy him, his capacity to hate. Like one envies a talent to sing I envy his capacity to hate. Damn him!

He shouts into the wind.

Damn you, Striven, you have torn me apart. You have…

HILARY stops abruptly, as though he's understood.

He has pieced the words together.

Below, don't forget, shout out. Don't forget, shout out 'below'.

He has remembered.

Yes. Those words. I know now. Oh my God! Oh my God! Don't forget, shout out 'below'! Oh my dear God!

The word 'below' is repeated and echoed like a recurrent tune in the head.

The thud.

The cry of pain.

The sound of swelling rain and wind.

Part Two – The Story

AN OLD WAREHOUSE

THE TIME: HILARY's student days. He's been assigned the job of a carpenter's mate working during his holidays with builders repairing a roof.

Lunch break.

TOM: You what they've sent me?

YOUNG HILARY: Afraid so.

TOM: 'Fraid so, are you? Well let's 'ope *I* won't be afraid so. You done this before?[1]

YOUNG HILARY: Not carpenter's mate but building sites plenty.

TOM: You a student?

HILARY: Afraid so.

TOM: 'Fraid so, 'fraid so! You better not be 'afraid so' of too many things or you'll be no good to me, Cocker. We climb ladders in this job, swing on roofs, rock in cradles and slide along 'igh rafters. I don't want no crying and no jelly-livers and no 'fraid sos alongside me. You got that?

YOUNG HILARY: You won't have to worry on my account, Mister –

TOM: You can call me Tom, but that don't mean you can take liberties. I may look only a little older than you and I can see you've got bleedin' clever eyes and I can 'ear your mouth is full of clever books but I'm the chippy on the job and I've got the know-'ow and you see these 'ands? They've got nearly ten years carpentry in them so what

---

[1]   Cockney dialect is familiar to actors and so I've only hinted at it by dropping Tom's aitches. It would make tiresome reading to write 'things' 'fings' and 'thoughts' 'fawts' etc

I say goes and that's a thing you and me better get clear from the start. Got that, Mister –

YOUNG HILARY: I think so. And you can call me Hilary.

> *RON KIMBER and his young mate RORY arrive with their lunch packs.*

TOM: 'E says we can call 'im 'Ilary. This 'ere's Ron Kimble, plumber on the job and the 'andsomest plumber this side of the Atlantic which you'll 'ave proof of 'cos you'll see the way girls and women look at 'im but, I'll say this for 'im, it don't spoil him, do it, china? 'E turns 'is 'ead and gets on with the job and 'e's a pleasure to work with. And this 'ere is Rory, 'is mate. Be careful of Rory, 'e makes mistakes.

RORY: He's right!

RON: Don't ever do nothing right do yer, matey?

RORY: Right! Right! There's nothing I do isn't a balls up. *(To YOUNG HILARY.)* I'll swap half a cheese-and-chutney for one of your boiled eggs.

YOUNG HILARY: Done!

RORY: But I try. I do try, don't I, Ron? Can't say I don't try. I know what has to be done, I've seen you do it a hundred times but the minute I put my hand to a job – smash! It's a jinx, like night blindness which me brother suffers from. But God knows I do try.

TOM: Well there'd better be no jinx this time because the job we're doing is clearing the roof of bluey.

> *All turn to see what YOUNG HILARY's reaction will be.*

> *He's not quite sure what they're talking about.*

RON: He knows what bluey is, don't he?

TOM: You know what bluey is, don't you?

YOUNG HILARY: Lead.

TOM: 'E knows what bluey is.

RON: Does he know the score?

TOM: 'E's only just been sent by the yard, leave off!

RORY: Is he a good boy, that's what we need to know. Is he a good and upright lad?

TOM: Leave 'im 'ave 'is lunch in peace. 'E's not yet lifted a tool in 'is 'and. Right, now, Master 'Ilary, lunch is thirty minutes but you take your time. The trick is not to do too much too fast or they'll expect you to do more, faster.

> *Though the next exchange is between the incumbents it's meant for YOUNG HILARY's ears.*

The bluey on this job is too old too dry and too cracked to save, right, Ron?

RON: Right, Tom.

TOM: But old and cracked and dry though it is –

RON: – it's gold dust.

TOM: Right, Ron, bleedin' gold dust. Now, what me and my new mate 'ere will do is cut it in strips, roll it, and knock it as flat as we can. *(To YOUNG HILARY.)* Got that?

YOUNG HILARY: Not sure yet.

TOM: Law a difficult thing to study?

YOUNG HILARY: For me it is.

TOM: Bit dim, are you?

YOUNG HILARY: Afraid so.

TOM: *(To the others.)* This bloke's afraid of everything.

RON: If he's afraid of everything he'll fail at everything. What made you choose law anyway?

YOUNG HILARY: My mother. She wanted a lawyer in the family.

TOM: Wanted an honest man about the 'ouse?

YOUNG HILARY: A rich and successful one, I think.

RORY: Isn't your family rich then?

YOUNG HILARY: Would I be working in my holidays if I were rich?

TOM: Oh, so you're family ain't rich then. Oh well, I mean, in my book all clever people is rich ain't they, Ron?

RORY: I'll swap half a pickle-and-ham for half a cheese-and-tomato.

YOUNG HILARY: Done.

RON: Glad we're not clearing this lead in winter time.

TOM: The yard'll make a packet out of this lot.

RON: I love working lead.

TOM: Gold dust. Like bleedin' gold dust.

RON: They die mining it but I love handling it.

TOM: Bleedin' better'n gold dust in fact.

RON: You can make lead go round things, mould it how you want.

TOM: A lunch bag each of this and we'd all 'ave a couple of quid in our pocket.

RON: Solid but pliable. Makes me wish I'd been a sculptor.

TOM: What d'yer think?

RORY: Now then! Putting criminal thoughts in the head of a judge what's to be.

TOM: 'E's not a judge yet and from what he tells me 'e could do with a couple of quid in 'is pocket.

RORY: I don't think you should go corrupting your mate, chippy. That's no way to start a young man off in life – a young man with such clever eyes. I'll swap you half an apple for half a pear.

YOUNG HILARY: Done.

RON: How long do you think the lead's lain there, Tom?

TOM: Gawd knows! A lot more years than you and me will ever see.

> *They're still waiting to see how YOUNG HILARY is interpreting all this.*

YOUNG HILARY: Tom.

TOM: Yes, china?

YOUNG HILARY: I think I understand what you're all planning to do.

TOM: What's that then, china?

YOUNG HILARY: You're planning to stash some of the lead from the roof and sell it.

TOM: We'll cut you in.

YOUNG HILARY: I'm not looking for a cut. But if you know that I know, it'll save you being embarrassed.

TOM: Embarrassed?

YOUNG HILARY: Crafty.

TOM: Crafty?

YOUNG HILARY: Circumspect!

TOM: Oh, I do like *that* word. Oh yes. That's a wealth of a word that one. It tells you what it means straight away, don't it? Circumspect! So, you ain't aiming to tell no one?

YOUNG HILARY: I'm in and out of jobs like this all the time. It's not my right.

TOM: No lectures on thievery and rogues and wrong-doing and pure living and conscience and things?

Pause.

That's my old china. Liked your face as soon as you come into this warehouse. Those bleedin' clever eyes.

RON: We can spell it out now then, can't we?

TOM: Indeed we can. So – 'ere's the plan. We've got to be very 'circumspect'. Rory takes up watch. Ron stands by with our four packs. 'Ilary and me – up inside the window which will be conveniently left open by your's truly, and up the ladder which will be left conveniently in the right place also by your's truly. 'Ilary will shift the bluey from under the corrugated sheets to the ledge. I'll whistle once to make sure Ron's in place, and then Ron – that 'andsomest of plumbers – will whistle back. Then, I'll yell 'below', count three, drop it over the edge, whistle. Yell 'below', count three, drop, whistle, and so on. Everyone understand?

RORY: It's very clever of you to put me on lookout. Can't do anything wrong just looking out, can I? I mean, I just stand around and look out. Simple!

RON: You *could* fall asleep.

The lights slowly fade to blue.

What follows is heard through the dimness.

TOM: Right, we're off. Jesus Christ! This ladder's not secure. Rope's loose. Must fix that. Now mind you don't fall. Everything's different in the dark.

Pause.

TOM whistles.

RON returns the whistle.

TOM's call is whispered –

Below – ow – ow – ow! *(To himself.)* One, two, three – over she goes.

Dull thud of lead landing.

Pause.

TOM whistles.

RON whistles.

Below – ow – ow – ow! *(To himself.)* One, two, three – over she goes.

Dull thud of lead landing.

Pause.

TOM whistles. No response. Whistles again. No response.

What's 'olding 'im? *(Calling.)* Ron – you alright?

RON: The last lump's too big. I'm cutting it into smaller pieces. You'll have to hang on a bit.

TOM: 'Ilary. You can throw the next one, I'm going to tighten the rope on the ladder. Wait for Ron's whistle, and don't forget, shout out 'below', count three, and then 'eave over. Got that.

YOUNG HILARY: Got it.

TOM: You're very cool about it. It's like you've lifted bluey every day of the week. You sure you ain't never stolen nothing before?

YOUNG HILARY: I used to steal sweets from Woolworths as a kid. Creep around picking them out between the glass joins.

TOM: Wicked!

YOUNG HILARY: I once kept a book from the library and said I'd lost it.

TOM: Wicked! Wicked!

YOUNG HILARY: And sometimes I'd pinch pennies from my mother's handbag.

TOM: Wicked! Wicked! Wicked! I'm off. You OK?

YOUNG HILARY: OK.

>*Pause.*

>*RON whistles.*

>*HILARY whistles.*

YOUNG HILARY: *(To himself.)* One, two, three – over she goes.

>*A horrifying scream.*

HILARY'S STUDY

HILARY: *(In great distress.)* I didn't shout 'below'. I whistled, I counted three but I forgot to shout 'below'. I forgot it! I forgot it! Oh, God help me, I forgot to shout 'below'.

>*Sound of rain, of wind. Swells and recedes.*

And when I did, he looked up just in time to see the jagged lump that was about to hit him. What happened next? I've forgotten what happened next. Did we call an ambulance? Did Tom walk him to a hospital? All I can remember is he said 'clear away the bluey before anyone comes.' Did I hear him say that or do I remember being *told* that's what he said? There was a conversation…

THE WAREHOUSE

>*TOM and YOUNG HILARY.*

TOM: I've been to see 'im. Not pretty. Ward sister tell me 'e'll be alright but not for a while yet. Concussion. Bloody 'ell! Lucky 'e wasn't killed, lump of lead like that. Lucky for you too, cocker…

>*Pause.*

'Course 'e didn't *say* it was a lump of lead. Said it was some slates and bricks the wind blew off a building site coming 'ome from the pub. 'E was very circumspect about it. *(Beat.)* I tell 'im we couldn't sell the stuff after that.

(Beat.) I tell 'im we took it back to the yard. *(Beat.)* Poor sod! Don't think 'e took much in. Or really cared.

He's watching YOUNG HILARY closely.

Only 'ave to split the money three ways now.

YOUNG HILARY's distress turns to rage.

YOUNG HILARY: What? Split the money three ways? The man's lying in hospital concussed and you're thinking of doing him out of the money? You tawdry, contemptible, lying, cheating monster, you! You're thinking of the money? The *money?* Yes, you split it three ways! And you make sure he's the third. You make fucking sure that poor man gets his money, you hear me? You make sure or I'll tell the whole fucking world about the bluey job. You hear me?

HILARY'S STUDY

HILARY: But what did I do after that? Nothing, I can remember nothing. I can't even remember climbing down off the roof. What did I say to Ron Kimble? Was I involved in confirming the lies to anybody? Did I check that Tom had shared the money with the plumber? Why can't I remember? I can't see faces, I can't see settings, dear God! I can't even remember visiting him in hospital. And what happened to him? Was he scarred for life? That handsomest of plumbers this side of the Atlantic – whatever happened to him?

The sound of the wind and rain swells.

HILARY moves to –

THE LONDON KITCHEN

SOPHIE: You look dreadful, Hilary. Your face is drawn and thin and you have dark rings round your eyes. Dreadful. This is no way to recover. You've solved the riddle of the disjointed phrases, the doctor has passed you fit – what more do you want? I'm not being unsympathetic but you don't eat enough or regularly, and your introspection is morbid and indulgent. Frankly, Hilary, you're a brooding and unhappy presence in the house. Most men would be thrilled with early retirement – catch up on books, hobbies, travel. You? Look at you! Haunted! Dreadful!

HILARY: I'm sorry, Sophie, you're right. Forgive me but I … I…

SOPHIE: *(More tenderly.)* Hilary, this is not you. To be brought down by the past? You? Who've seen so many skeletons in other people's cupboards. Talk with friends, ask them to share a guilt or two. Don't be so harsh on yourself. It was an accident. Believe me, darling, if mankind boasted no more wickedness than that…

He rises and reaches to put on his overcoat.

SOPHIE: Don't go back to Wales. Please, Hilary. I don't care what ascetics say, solitude is unnatural. There's no health in those hills if your heart's heavy and your mind's tormented. You don't even feed yourself! You can't reflect in isolation, not really reflect. Thought eats thought. Self-hatred feeds upon itself. You won't lay old ghosts you'll simply conjure up new ones. Listen to me, Hilary, stay among people.

But he moves to –

HILARY'S STUDY

HILARY: Too many sins of omission. Clogged up the arteries with rusty old errors. Calcified the heart with small deceits. And the Strivens of this world make me unfit for the company of wives.

How could I have lived all my life not knowing how a man I've damaged lived his.

(Singing.)

My uncle he was a Spanish Captain...

There was a time I could identify wrong, when I thought punishment could redeem. I could carry the law, the land, and my loved ones like a featherweight of flowers. Easy.

Wish I could give up writing this diary. Who do I write for?

(Singing.)

My uncle he was a Spanish Captain
Went to sea a month ago...

He stumbles.

Better sit. What was I singing for? Don't usually sing to myself. Strange feeling. Floating. Dizzy. Weak. Haven't eaten. Three days without food. Penance! I'm doing penance for you, Ron Kimble. Don't feel ill, though, just – high. Bit delirious perhaps. Quite pleasant, actually. Not much of a penance to be pleasantly high.

(Singing.)

My uncle he was a Spanish Captain
Went to sea a month ago
First he kissed me then he left me
Bade me always answer no
Oh no John no John no John no.

> *Over this is the wind and a ghostly voice which seems to be whispering 'look for me, look for me, keep looking, keep looking for me'.*
>
> *The howl of the wind grows. HILARY's distress rises above it.*

Do you wonder about me, Ron Kimble? Because I wonder about you. Where are you? What happened to your life? Are you philosophical, bitter, did you marry, did you have children, were you scarred for life, did you become ugly, live alone, full of hatred? I've questions for you, Ron Kimble, so many questions, so much I need to know.

The wind and ghostly voice fade.

Part Three – The Quest

HILARY will meet four people who will lead him to RON KIMBLE.

But he will never confront RON. He will only fantasise three possible confrontations.

TOM'S FRONT ROOM

Old now.

TOM: I don't believe it. I don't believe it. You don't 'ave to tell me 'oo you are. I know 'oo you are. I'd know 'oo you are anywhere, anytime, any age. Those bleedin' clever eyes and a mouth full of clever books. Well! This is an honour, your honour.

HILARY: You've got a comfortable old age I see, Tom.

TOM: Worked hard, didn't I! You've not done so badly, either.

HILARY: Worked hard, didn't I!

> *They exchange smiles and awkward silences.*

TOM: But you don't look 'appy.

HILARY: I'm a troubled man, Tom.

TOM: Ain't we all.

HILARY: Do you remember Ron Kimble?

TOM: I wondered what it was brought you 'ere. Didn't think it was old Tom's life you was interested in.

HILARY: Did you ever give him his share of that money?

TOM: I did. And you've got to believe that. Straight! I *did* give 'im his share of the money 'cos you put the fear of God up me. Straight! Even then. Cor! I shouldn't like to be before you as a judge now.

HILARY: And do you know what happened to him when he came out of hospital?

TOM: Worked. Like all of us had to.

HILARY: Was he –

TOM: Scarred for life? The 'andsomest plumber this side of the Atlantic? Well, it weren't ever gonna fade away.

HILARY is distressed.

HILARY: Do you think he could be traced?

TOM: I don't 'ave an address but I did see him once or twice, in an area by the warehouses near where we worked. Remember? It's all changed now. Saint Katherine's docks. Shops, galleries, big 'otel – you seen it? In that area…

MONTGOMERY FRONT DOOR

MRS MONTGOMERY: No, no one name of Kimble lives here. No one name of Kimble lived here *before* us, either. Name of Montgomery lives here now, and the name of Mitchum lived here before us. I can tell you where the Mitchum's live if you want to know because the Mitchum's live round the corner in a bigger house. That's why they moved from here. They kept having children and so this house got too small for them and they moved to number eighty-three Larchmont Road. I know they moved there 'cos we helped them move…

MITCHUM FRONT DOOR

MRS MITCHUM: Kimble? Kimble? No, no one by that name lived in King Street when *we* moved in there. Their name was Morgan and the Morgan's didn't move anywhere because they got killed poor things in a car crash which was funny old fate if you think about it since he built his own car with his own hands! Took eighteen months to construct his own coffin, you might say. Funny old life.

KATIE'S DELICATESSEN

KATIE: Come in, sir, come in. We got lots more goodies inside, so you keep looking. The only Jewish delicatessen shop left this side of the East End but they come from miles around to old Katie's because old Katie was featured in the Sunday Times colour supplement. See? *(Showing him.)* Nice picture, eh? Keep looking! Keep looking!

HILARY starts at this last phrase.

You're not a Jewish gent and I've never seen you before so what brings you here? The Sunday Times piece?

HILARY: No. I – I'm not sure. I was just wandering...

KATIE: Sightseeing the East End?

HILARY: No, I –

KATIE: Nothing wrong with a bit of slumming. Interesting all-sorts you get here.

HILARY: No, I – I was – I mean I – I'm looking for someone.

KATIE: Then you've come to the right person because Katie remembers all her customers.

HILARY: No. I've not come into your shop looking for him.

KATIE: You've not?

HILARY: I've just... It was chance... Your window. It was so full of things. And then I looked inside...

KATIE: That's what I tell everyone to do – keep looking, keep looking!

HILARY: It's a strange phrase.

KATIE: Nothing strange about it, sir. I fill my deli with so many things that customers can't see everything immediately. So I tell them – keep looking, keep looking. *(Pause.)* A lost relative?

HILARY: No. Someone I worked with on a building site.

KATIE: You? A building site?

HILARY: My student days.

KATIE: Ah! Student days! Wish I'd had student days. *(Beat.)* Well, you're here now. Might as well give me his name.

HILARY: You couldn't possibly –

KATIE: Stranger things have happened.

HILARY: Kimble.

KATIE: Kimble?

HILARY: *(Spelling it.)* K-i-m-

KATIE: You don't have to spell it for me. Kimble. Ron Kimble.

HILARY: *(Incredulous.)* You know him?

KATIE: You don't forget the Ron Kimble's of this world, struck by the hand of God to carry his message to all corners telling us: never be sure of anything. God's like that, you know. Sometimes he does things too well and then regrets it. And Ron Kimble walks around – the living proof.

HILARY: Proof? Of what?

KATIE: Too handsome. No one should be as handsome as that. 'You're too handsome' God said. And then struck. The right side you can still fall in love with but the left – well, you'll see. Like a huge beast had scratched him. Deep scars. Angry. I'm a great believer in God's justice and the ways of fate. I mean who do you think guided you to Katie's who does special dishes for Ron Kimble? Cream cheese, smoked salmon bagels, pickled cucumbers which I pickle myself with a special recipe my old mother handed on to me from Poland, and chopped liver. He loves my chopped liver. Sometimes he wants hot soups, barley soups, knadellech soups.

> *Pause to regard him.*

You don't know what I'm talking about do you?

128

He doesn't.

Now, you go out here and you first turn left, then by a pub called The Mason's Arms you'll find…

KIMBLE'S FRONT DOOR/FRONT ROOM

HILARY watches RON and imagines him addressing the spirit of himself who should have been standing there.

FIRST RON: You? I forget your name but – you? Well, strike me dead! *(Laughs.)* You nearly did, didn't you? Ha! That's a joke – 'strike me dead!' You!

You're a judge, ain't you? Remember the first time I see your photo in the paper I said I know that face. It was the eyes. Young Tom used to call you 'bleedin' clever-eyes'. There's a lot of water passed under the bridge since then, eh?

Come to see old scar-face? Come to see how 'the handsomest of plumbers' survived? Well, I can't grumble. I was scarred but I wasn't maimed. Could have lost a hand on a blow-lamp in our trade, couldn't we, or fallen off a ladder and broke me back? I'm a bit of a sight to look at, and age don't help, but I've got me health, and as you can see from me flat I ain't bad off. Blimey! You do look pale.

Tell you what. It's only the afternoon, I know, but how about a spot of whisky? What'll your blood say to that? Bring a bit of colour to your cheeks this will. The best. Glenmorangie. Spoil meself. We don't want to go remembering rotten old times. I didn't have a full life, not a full family life like others but it was a sort of a life. Even travelled a bit. Plumbed on liners to sunny places. And I've seen poverty and misery makes *my* life seem like it was spent in heaven.

HILARY is crying.

You crying? You mustn't cry. That's not a manly thing to do, your honour, not for someone in your position. And what for? I didn't much cry for meself so I don't have no need of your tears.

SECOND RON: *(Cry of rage.)* Out! Get out! You value your life you'll get out. Out! Out! Out! You won't? Right! See this wire brush, see it? If you're not out by the time I count three, I'll have this down the left side of your face. One. Two. Three. Out! Get out!

His rage subsides.

You knew, didn't you? You cocky bastard, clever eyes, you knew I couldn't do it. Though God knows how you knew 'cos there's many a time I imagined meeting you or looking you up and it was only with murder in my heart, I promise you.

What have you come for? Say sorry? Offer me compensation now you're a rich and famous judge? Why now? Why not when I was in torment 'cos I knew I'd never find a wife and never have a family and me friends were gone and me spirit and me hope for things?

And how did you find me? Eh? Of course! The lords of the land have access to all things. You can look up your files and ask friends in high places.

No. It was Katie wasn't it? But how did you get to *her*? Oh well, it don't matter, do it? Not any of it. Life's over. When you retire life's over anyway.

HILARY is crying.

No good *you* crying, mate. It's me got things to cry for. Ha! Listen to him. *He's* crying…

THIRD RON: Can't say I see you properly. Lost me sight, see. Had an accident made everything blurred. That's why the place is in such a mess so you'll have to excuse it. Can you find somewhere to sit in all this rubbish? I have someone come in and clean up once a week but I can't see what she does. As long as the main things are in place so's I can find me way around and there's a smell of lavender polish, I don't mind. Lavender polish! Must have the smell of lavender polish about the place.

Hilary Hawkins you say your name is? Can't honestly say I remember a Hilary Hawkins. Can't honestly say I remember anything much. Work in the legal profession, do you? What you come and see me for? I done something wrong? Funny thing, that. I tell you what I do wrong, mister, I go on living, that's what I do wrong. I go on and on and on and on, much as I'd like not to. I mean would *you* want to go on living like this?

Some old people round here I meet them sometimes and they tell me, they tell me they wake up in the mornings and they say 'well, thank God I made it to another day'. Not me. I wake up from darkness into semi-darkness and I say, 'Oh hell!' I say, 'not another day.' I wake up and I say, 'God help me, I've got to go through this lot again.' I wake up and I say, 'Bloody Christ! The dream's over.' Every day for forty years the dream's been over for me.

> *HILARY is crying.*

What's that whimpering? You hear whimpering? Where's it coming from, I wonder? Can you hear it? Sounds like a child's crying in a corner, done something wrong and gone into a corner to get out the way of punishment. Open that door. See if you can see someone. Here, sonny! Here, little boy! Don't cry! You can't go through life expecting never to do anything wrong. Come here to old scar-face. I've got some chocolate here. You come an' tell old scar-face about it, he'll put it right. He'll tell you about the world and things. Once upon a time there was the most handsomest plumber this side of the Atlantic…

> *He controls his weeping.*

> *To SOPHIE –*

HILARY: Nobody who's unhappy should assume responsibility of any kind – neither to teach nor judge nor advise. Unhappy people shouldn't advise friends nor have opinions nor write books nor be lovers nor have children.

SOPHIE: Don't go back to Wales, Hilary. Please. You'll just sit at your desk as you've sat over the years listening to the rain, wondering if it'll ever stop, writing your diary, trying to glue together a cracked life. Don't you *know* what an exterminating angel loneliness is?

HILARY'S STUDY

He stands by his desk.

Sound of wind and rain.

HILARY: I did *not* visit the handsomest plumber this side of the Atlantic. I just watched him shopping at Katie's, chatting with neighbours, giving sweets to children. And at his door he stood, looked out into the street as though for the last time and then turned back into his world. A destroyed life.

He sits to his desk, raises his pen, writes.

Ghosts like that can never be laid. Nothing will assuage the reproach. No! The remorse. No! The pain.

I sit here as I have sat over the years...

Sound of rain and wind.

Fade.

The End.

MEN DIE WOMEN SURVIVE

a play in two acts

28 scenes

Characters

MINERVA
a business woman, aged 50

MISCHA
an academic, aged 42

CLAIRE
political researcher, aged 39

The three male characters
are all played by one actor

MONTCRIEFF
aged 55, a writer, who left his wife, Minerva

LEO
aged 44, a financial analyst,
who was left by his wife, Mischa

VINCENT
aged 40, shadow cabinet minister, Scottish,
who left his mistress, CLAIRE.

Settings and Relationships

Four areas.

The largest, MISCHA LOWENTHAL's apartment.
Eclectic but exquisite taste.

She and her two friends, CLAIRE HOPE and MINERVA
THOMPSON, have gathered for a meal.

Three other areas surround the central one. They will be occupied
by the one actor playing each of the women's men whose names
are MONTCRIEFF, VINCENT, and LEO.

LEO's space: a hint of garden, garden shed,
garden bench, lawn mower.

MISCHA left him six months ago but he refuses to accept her
absence, imagines she's always there in the house, talks to her.

VINCENT's space: section of a TV studio.

He is being interviewed.
A married man, he has just ended an affair with CLAIRE.

Looming at an upper level is MONTCRIEFF's space:
hint of a study.

He's MINERVA's ex-husband; left her five years ago, talks to
someone off stage who's not there - his idealised mistress.

The women have gathered to share a three-course meal each part of which one of them has elaborately prepared.

They will talk about their dish and the wine they have chosen to accompany it but the scenes will be so arranged that the actors will have no need to be seen eating and the plates will be empty. Their descriptions will suffice.

Necessity requires that the opening of the play reveal its joints: the actor playing all three men must be seen changing from one character to another.

Clarity requires a kind of prologue*, a stylised opening in which the women reveal who they are and their relationship to the men – without it an audience's attention is distracted trying to work out who is who.

When the play opens all three WOMEN are in place in MISCHA's apartment in line with the spaces of their men.

* Though not, definitely not addressed to the audience.

Act One

Light on MISCHA.

MISCHA: I'm Mischa Lowenthal, lecturer in Hebrew studies.
I left my husband, Leo, a stockbroker, six months ago –
birth!

SCENE ONE

Garden.

*LEO, professionally strong and able but emotionally
adrift.*

LEO: *(Calling.)* MISCHAAAAAAAA.

> *He has hauled out a lawn mower from the shed,
> confronts it like a strange beast he's never before
> encountered.*
>
> *Remembers you need to pull out a choke. Does so.
> Next remembers the pull start. Jerks it once, twice,
> three times, to no avail.*
>
> *Sits, easily defeated, exhausted, bewildered.*
>
> *A thought, like a slowly gathering storm, is
> assembling in his mind.*

LEO: The universe is a ball
    bounced by a child
    living on a planet
    placed in a universe bounced
    by a child
    living on a planet
    placed in a universe bounced
    by a child
    living on a planet
    placed in a universe bounced

by a child
living on a planet…

> *Finds the image a gloomy one.*
>
> *Looks up.*

You gave me that, Lord. Don't blame me.

> *Thoughts, memories overwhelm him.*
>
> *Cries out again –*

MISCHAAAAAAAA!

> *Takes control of himself.*
>
> *Speaks to his wife rather than the Lord.*

Sorry. You don't like shouting. I know. Forgive me.

I'll get over it. Don't worry, Mischa. Husbands survive desertion. We're left bruised but we survive. Only it takes time.

I remember, you used to ask me: 'what one, unexpected thing would you like to do in your life? You're a financial analyst for a big stock-broking firm but what' you asked 'is the one secret thing you've really always wanted to do. Something *really* surprising.'

And I never knew what to reply. Used to drive you mad, I know, but what could I do, Mischa? I just didn't have a secret ambition. Forgive me.

> *Softer.*

Mischaaaaaaaa!

> *Lights up on MINERVA.*

MINERVA: Minerva Thompson, a businesswoman, ex-wife of Montcrieff Hardy, a writer, he left me five years ago – chaos.

SCENE TWO

MONTCRIEFF's study.

MONTCRIEFF: And she blackmailed me with it, my wife, Minerva. 'I had the pain you had the pleasure.' But I didn't want the pleasure, I wanted the pain. I *wanted* to have babies. Yes, my love – birth! More than anything in the world I wanted to give birth, my own children, not be dependent on the blackmailing female of the tribe.

Are you listening in there? If we're to become new partners in life you must know about me. I don't only want to give birth to a literary masterpiece I also want to give birth to a life.

What's that you say? Too late? Men can't give birth after fifty? You're right! And didn't she know it. 'Men can't give birth after fifty' she mocked. Taunted me with my limitations. 'I had the pain you had the pleasure.' An emotional terrorist, my wife. Leading light of the women's mafia. The Godmother!

Lights up on CLAIRE.

CLAIRE: Claire Hope…political researcher…Vincent Ferguson…a mistress…pain.

SCENE THREE

TV studio.

VINCENT preparing to be interviewed.

VINCENT: Yes, I know the questions become very personal at the end. I'm one of the millions who gawp at your program. You're quite merciless on occasions. But I think I can cope, I've nothing to hide. Though I'm not ashamed to admit, I'd sooner face my opposite in the House of Commons than face that evil eye there. How's my tie? I can never get my tie right. First the wide end's too long then the thin end's too long. I tie and untie a dozen times before they come equal. Or nearly equal. The wide end always has to be a wee bit longer, I'm aware of that. I'm jabbering aren't I? I'm aware of that too. Nerves. I'll be all right though. Once your camera's turning and you're asking me difficult questions I'll be away. This idiot you see before you will turn into an oracle, a sage and wit of the kind we in Scotland produce endlessly much to the envy and chagrin of the English who are cool, calculating and boring – I promise. Does the light have to shine so brightly?

SCENE FOUR

MISCHA's apartment.

MINERVA, decanting a bottle of red wine.

MISCHA, laying the table.

CLAIRE, rubbing with a cloth, wine glasses to shine. She seems obsessive.

MINERVA: Men! They're all the same! Interchangeable!

Pause.

Look at the colour of this wine.

Pause.

And they're incapable of making decisions.

Pause.

Now there, sisters, is a colour speaks of passion. Just look.

Holds it to the light for them to see, slightly tipping the glass.

And no drop. Clings with confidence to the glass.

They hover. Have you noticed? Men hover, like birds before a window-pane, fluttering their poor wings at reflections instead of the real world. No comprehension of what they're looking at.

There's this marvellous cartoon of a vast woman with a fully dressed city gent over her shoulder. He hangs there, ecstatically, his briefcase still in his hand. And she's saying to him: 'Now, burp!'

She holds up the decanter to continue pouring.

MINERVA: Regard! Centuries of good earth and the summer of '55 soaked up there. Enough to make you believe in God. You'll know all about heaven after a glass of that.

She places decanter in the middle of table.

Flutter and hover! You have to make all the decisions *for* them so that when you finally kick them out they can say '*you* did it! *you* closed the door' which, as you, I and all the world knows is the way my bold ex-husband, Montcrieff, explained it happened.

MISCHA: Montcrieff? I thought you hated Hardy being called Montcrieff.

MINERVA: That was when I loved him.

MISCHA: Strange names parents give their children.

CLAIRE: Well Mischa isn't exactly everyday nomenclature.

MISCHA: It was where *my* parents were born.

MINERVA: Have you got any middle names?

MISCHA: Stephania. The Jews name their children after dead relatives, never live ones. Stephania after my grandfather, Solomon; Mischa after my grandmother, Miriam.

They carry on their different tasks in silence.

MINERVA is trying to peel off the label from the wine bottle.

After some seconds –

MISCHA: *(To CLAIRE.)* Claire? Do *you* have other names to go between Claire and Hope?

CLAIRE: Dawn.

MISCHA: Nice.

MINERVA: Claire! Dawn! Hope!

CLAIRE: You've got it. My parents wanted all my dawn's to be 'claire' and my day's to be full of hope. They revealed it on my twenty-first birthday when they presented me with a necklace of twenty-one pearls which they'd bought one a year.

MISCHA: The schemes of our parents!

Continue in silence.

To MINERVA –

MISCHA: Minerva?

MINERVA: I was hoping you wouldn't ask.

MISCHA: We have done.

MINERVA: Minerva Avril Loretta Thompson.

Silence. The others cannot see what is wrong with the name.

MALT! I was a war baby. M – A – L – T. My parents swore by malt. *Please* lets change the subject. My parents are not my favourite people.

SCENE FIVE

MONTCRIEFF's study.

MONTCRIEFF: *No* one was really her favourite person. Except me. I was the centre of her life. That was her downfall. But I was wild, full of appetites and divine discontent, the kind of man women find a challenge. Like cowboys tame wild horses certain women are driven to tame wild men.

(Calling.) Are you listening? Are you there, my dream girl, my lucky find, my once-in-a-lifetime lover?

I could never understand why Shakespeare created a
Katarina to be tamed by a Petrucio. Got it wrong again
didn't he? Got Richard Three wrong; got de ole black man
wrong; got the Jew wrong, oi! And women! Except in love.
He knew about love and passion. Ah! Old Will! Where
there's a will there's a play!

But tame me she could not, my ex! 'Frivolous! Infantile!
Failed!' she scoffed. I am not, I hasten to assure you,
entirely failed – I do make a living as a writer. And not
entirely frivolous either. Not English enough to be entirely
frivolous. Have you observed the neurotic drive of the
English to be ever flippant? Tiresome, don't you think? Or
are you irretrievably English? Perhaps you're not English
at all but completely, utterly, helplessly foreign! Or English
with foreign extractions? I don't really know what you
look like. Blonde? Brunette? Grey? *(Pause.)* Black? White?
Asiatic?

> *Pause.*

Would you like me to cook for you? It's true I can't have
babies but I'm a very good cook, and when you get broody
I will get broody and I'll look after you wonderfully.

> *Pause.*

She will answer me one day won't she?

> *Mind wanders.*

SCENE SIX

> *MISCHA's apartment. Everything is prepared for
> the meal.*

MINERVA: Now. We're agreed. No cocktails. Just drink with
the meals. And we each talk about the dish we've prepared
and the wine we've selected *before* we eat.

MISCHA: Agreed!

MINERVA: Claire?

CLAIRE is distrait. The others are aware of her state.
The meal is not the reason why they have assembled.

Claire Dawn Hope?

CLAIRE: Agreed.

MINERVA: And then – men! We are gathered, dearly beloved, to talk about men, especially your Leo, her Vincent and my 'Mont-bloody-crieff', and to help Claire face desertion!

MISCHA: We are here 'dearly beloved' to eat a good meal and help Claire *if* Claire wants help. Claire might even change her mind and want to watch Vincent being interviewed on tele.

MINERVA: Don't be daft! It was bad enough she had to deny being his mistress.

CLAIRE: Please! Let us agree not to talk about Vincent.

MISCHA: Did they have any suspicions?

MINERVA: They probed a bit, hoping for dirt. Even if she hadn't been his mistress the researchers would have thought she was. Never work with pretty women!

MISCHA: I think he's insane. No one's ever come away from that interview unscathed.

MINERVA: First they lull you into false security so's you imagine you've got the interviewer eating out of your hands and then – crash! bang! Down come careers, families, a life's work… But our saint here remained loyal to her bastard despite all.

MISCHA: Vincent's not a bastard, he's an old friend who's impetuous, needs constant cautioning and I should have talked him out of it. *(To CLAIRE.)* *You* should have talked him out of it, Claire.

CLAIRE: Can we please change the subject.

MISCHA: Yes, but not to talk about what women are supposed to talk about when they get together.

MINERVA: You will before the evening's out I promise you, there will be no pussyfooting around this dinner table.

MISCHA: Can I remind you that it is *my* dinner table?

CLAIRE: That's how her business flourishes.

MISCHA: She was always Miss Bossy Pants.

MINERVA: Now don't start talking about me as though I wasn't here, and let me say in my defence with no concession to modesty – for I can see it is to become an evening of 'no holds barred' and I may be in for a rough time – that, though I am often judgemental, and who isn't – I am also loved, admired, depended upon and the softest touch in town.

So. Let's start with Mischa's hors-d'oeuvre. What is it, what wine is it to go with, and why?

MISCHA: I wanted to visit the land where the cedars come from before I began translating the Song of Songs –

MINERVA: – which is Solomon's –

MISCHA: – which is *not* Solomon's. Ernest Renan who, as you probably know, was the eminent 'membre de L'Academie Francaise' and wrote a celebrated Life of Jesus, also –

MINERVA: No! I probably *don't* know! I can't bear it when people assume I share their erudite, cultural framework. My father was a ticket collector, I *have* no cultural framework, and I'm –

CLAIRE: I hope she doesn't plan to say she's proud of it.

MINERVA: Oh you're still alive then?

> *MISCHA smothers the moment before it grows.*

MISCHA: Ernest Renan also put forward the theory that the Song of Songs is not really a long poem by Solomon but a kind of play *about* Solomon. About Solomon and a Shulamite shepherdess who was *abducted* by Solomon when he saw her tending the vineyards one day. Far from loving Solomon she's really very unimpressed with him and longs for her true love who is a shepherd.

CLAIRE: In my teens I had a boyfriend used to quote verses from The Song of Songs. Used to stroke my belly round and round and recite:

'Thou art beautiful, oh my love, as Tirzah,
comely as Jerusalem' –

MISCHA: – says Solomon to his Shulamite, and then he adds *'terrible as an army with banners'*. Now why does he add that? Why does he tell her she is as terrible as an army with banners? Renan thinks the answer lies further down in verse 12 of chapter 6.

'I went down into the garden of nuts to see the
fruits of the valley and to see whether the vine
flourished, and the pomegranates budded.
' Or ever I was aware, my soul made me like the
chariots of Ammi-nadib.'

Oh fatal step! A visit to the vines and there she was – lifted into the chariot of a king's train.

MINERVA: Poor Shulamite! Plunged into the arms of lecherous old Solomon!

CLAIRE: How do you know her shepherd wasn't a lecher, or wouldn't become one.

MINERVA: We'll come to you, Claire, when the time is right. So, Mischa, The Song of Songs, Solomon and – ?

MISCHA plunks wine on the table.

MISCHA: And red wine from Lebanon. Kosraia '64!

MINERVA: Why Lebanon?

MISCHA: Solomon made himself a chariot of the wood of
Lebanon. His palace was in Lebanon. The shepherd tells
his Shulamite love: '...*and the smell of thy garments is like
the smell of Lebanon...*' So, I had to see Lebanon. The tiny
village of Kosraia, in the south, a lush, hilly area called
Alboukah.

MINERVA: And the hors d'ouvres?

MISCHA: I'd been walking all morning, before the sun became
too hot, and had to stop in a restaurant for a coffee and a
mid-morning snack. A little restaurateur – he spoke Arabic,
French and English – we began talking. And when I told
him that I was making a new translation of the Song of
Songs in the shape of a play, to my surprise he asked:
from which language – Hebrew or Latin? I told him,
Hebrew. 'You're Jewish?' he asked. 'I'm British' I said, 'but
a Hebrew scholar.' 'You're Jewish' he said, 'don't be afraid.
We all have our madmen. I'm not one of them. Here' he
said, and he took out a plate from his rusty, peeling old
fridge, 'here, a taste you will never taste anywhere else in
the world. I had it from my parents who had it from their
parents who had it from their parents all the way back
to Seulemen – Kibbey Nayeh. Fresh raw lamb, minced;
crushed wheat; raw onion, cut small, crisp; one beaten
egg; arabic sweet pepper; salt; and a local herb impossible
to buy here called Kamoun. I begged it from a Lebanese
restaurant in Piccadilly.

> *MISCHA pours out the wine. They raise their glasses
> to each other, drink, then turn their attention to
> 'the dish'.*

Taste!

SCENE SEVEN

LEO by garden shed, contemplating the lawn mower again – something he had always hated but must now confront.

Again pulls the cord, again it refuses to come alive. Has no idea what to do – never mowed a lawn before. Machines confuse him.

LEO: Gardeners! Why do employees fall ill?

Cups hands to face, and again cries to the air in desperation –

MISCHAAAAAAAA!

Long silence.

Calms down.

She stopped loving me, what could I do? Stopped! Ceased! Dried up! Childhood friends, thirteen years married, two children, and I became unlovable! Unloved any longer. Like this lawn mower. Though this lawn mower I never loved.

It's not a crime – to stop loving me. To stop loving me I could not say with my hand on my heart was a heinous crime. It's everyone's right to love, not to love, to love less, to stop loving.

But of course it was not so simple, because she liked me, perhaps even more than liked me. And why not? I was a good man – faithful, loyal, dependable! I'd given her the best years of my life, her beloved children, days of roses and wine and verse beneath the bough. Why shouldn't she like me a little, even a lot?

But love? That searing madness? That insatiable longing? That ache to be there all the time? That sharp nerve-end sharing of every domestic detail of the day: she watching him peel her an apple, him watching her drying her skin, she watching him shaving, swimming together, walking

together, listening to music, watching a movie, just holding
on to one another for the dear last years of life? None
of that. All that dead and gone. Affection in place of
passion.... Sad.... Sad and over.... Batteries run out.... Sing
lullabies for the day's end.... Sing lamentations.... For the
night has come....

SCENE EIGHT

MISCHA's apartment.

They have finished the hors-d'hoeuvre.

MINERVA: Oh my God! That was a taste to excite, and a wine
to weep for.

MISCHA: Come, it was an exquisite wine but no wine is to
weep for.

CLAIRE: Do you think only human beings are to weep for?

MISCHA: Mostly, yes.

CLAIRE: I once visited a stone garden in Kyoto that made me
weep.

We were there two years ago you'll remember – a
Parliamentary delegation trying to persuade the Japanese
to lift their trade barriers. He and I took off, as we often did
on such journeys, broke away – he needed to explore the
ceramics industry, he said. Kyoto.

We entered a temple. The temple of Ryoanji. He told
me to close my eyes, took me by the hand, led me, then
said 'open them'. It was a shock. Rocks, moss, furrows of
small stones. Laid out by two brothers six hundred years
ago. My eyes saw it, my stomach felt it. What? I never
know the word to use when I talk about it – rightness?
harmony? courage? All those things. But more. It was to do
with the unexpected. Those brothers had the courage to
imagine that a juxtaposition of the unexpected was right,

harmonious, perfect. It was the courage of the unexpected made me weep.

> *Of course she wants to weep for her life going wrong. Restrains herself.*

MINERVA: I don't believe in perfection. Human *beings* aren't perfect and what they *produce* shouldn't be.

MISCHA: *Shouldn't* be? You're *dictating* imperfection?

MINERVA: *Can't* be, then.

> *'All things are literally better, lovelier, and more beloved for the imperfections which have been divinely appointed, that the law of human life may be effort, and the law of human judgement, mercy.*

> *Pause.*

Ruskin.

> *Pause.*

The Nature of the Gothic.

> *Pause. She feels she has to explain how she came by the quotations.*

(Sheepishly.) Evening Institute course on British Cathedrals… Cultural frameworks and all that!

> *Awkward silence.*

CLAIRE: I know a very funny story about an American football player called Puzaltski.

MISCHA: *You* know an American story? But there's no one more English county than you.

MINERVA: You don't *have* to hide behind laughter, Claire.

MISCHA: The English! We have this great need to defuse our emotions with giggles.

MINERVA: On the other hand – I need laughter. If I was given the choice between laughter and money I'd have no hesitation in choosing. I need laughter like I need oxygen.

Awkward silence.

CLAIRE: *'I charge you, O ye daughters of Jerusalem, by the roes, and by the hinds of the field, that ye stir not up, nor awake my love, until it pleases her'.*

MISCHA: *(Reminding them.)* Said the shepherd to the women of Solomon's harem.

CLAIRE: And he rubbed and he stroked and he rubbed and he stroked, in small circles, quoting without pause.

Silence.

I thought one was supposed not to decant good wine any longer.

MINERVA: Well, like Moses you supposes erroneously. It's impolite to leave wine in the bottle so that guests can see how expensively they're being hosted.

CLAIRE: Disagree. It's more polite to please your guests with information about what they're drinking. There's pleasure in labels.

MINERVA: *Visual* pleasures! I prefer tastes – like people – to come through with *out* labels.

SCENE NINE

TV studio.

VINCENT being interviewed.

VINCENT: There is no doubt in my mind that the three major issues to confront the 21st century will be world poverty, environment, and a conflict between believers and non-believers. Or, to be more optimistic, between countries driven by religious fanaticism and countries with a tradition of religious tolerance. But those are the chapter headings not the sub-headings, and it's the sub-headings which are crucial.

He pauses as though listening to an interviewer's question.

What do I mean by that? What I mean by that is – take the problem of the conflict between religious fanaticism and religious tolerance. Voltaire thought it was solved 250 years ago when the age of reason dawned over Europe, but reason and tolerance didn't, like spring, burst out all over. Now, why? We have to be able to identify the spiritual bacteria that inflames bigotry. Or do we just pacify religious states with a kind of soothing, there-there-we-love-you diplomacy? Is education the answer to fanaticism? Or must we make damn sure we've got a good military defence against holy wars?

Here's a formulation which I think should be printed as huge posters and stuck on walls all over the world:

*My respect for your liberty to live and pray and believe as you wish does not mean I have to respect **what** you believe, **how** you live or the **content** of your prayers.*

Pause.

Listening.

Yes. I *am* a believer, believe it or not!

SCENE TEN

MISCHA's apartment.

MINERVA lays out three fondue sauces. 'Lights' the paraffin. Pours wine.

MINERVA: The bastard left me but he knew how to cook, and petty will I not be. The fondue, sisters, is the first meal he ever prepared for me and though I hate and despise his frivolous and infantile spirit yet will I honour the memory of his culinary skills.

You have before you one red, one green, one yellow sauce, these being the traditional colours of the fondue meal. My red is sour cream, reddened with a tomato paste, heated with a touch of cayenne pepper, chili and some drops of tabasco. My green is mousse of avocado with creme frache and drops of lemon. My yellow is as much to do with textures as tastes – mayonnaise which I made myself, mandarin slices – from the tin I'm afraid, and crushed walnuts. Sweet, crunchy, velvety, and softly fatty. On the small plates you will find raw mushrooms, raw onion, and slices of green pepper to spear with your beef which is – I promise you – best fillet no expense spared.

The wine comes to me from other sources and marks the end of my marriage. Between this fondue and this red wine stretches, sisters dear, a quarter of a century of married bliss and blood. Could a graph be drawn it would show a steady decline from the heights of unimaginably original passion to the lows of unbelievably original venom. By the end we were lacerating one another into emotional cubes which, like the meats we are about to deep-fry, we deep-fried in our very own and seething blue angers.

The details are banal, and just as banal was the fact that I loved him throughout. Until he left me. Then I hated him. To go through all that pain and misery and not reap the pleasures of hate? Not this sister, my sisters. I could forgive the bastard not.

Pause. Waiting for a sign.

And do I hear you ask me *how* I discovered the wine?

MISCHA: Our eyes, our eyes, look at our eager eyes for God's sake!

CLAIRE: *(Mocking.)* Wait we cannot!

> *MINERVA tells her story as though reading from a novel.*

MINERVA: He stood me up for a concert one night. It was Bernstein conducting Mahler. Sold out. A man was looking for a ticket. An American professor of physics. I sold him mine. We sat alongside each other saying nothing. Both of us afraid the other would mistake a word for a pass. Mahler flooded our emotions. At one moment I dared to glance at him. His eyes were closed. Ah! The sensitive soul I thought. Until his head thumped loose on my left shoulder. Jet lag! Here was a boy needing to be tucked up in bed not ravished by the chords of Jewish melancholy. I reassured him with the most sympathetic of my famed smiles. In the foyer he caught up with me.

'Could you direct me,' he asked with that special brand of mournful American courtesy, 'Could you direct me to the nearest Underground?'

'Where are you making for?' I, with absolutely no intention of taking him there, responded.

'The Westbury Hotel' he replied with the appeal of a lost and lonely visitor to strange lands.

'I'll take you there' I said, weakness overwhelming my poor old woman's resolve.

On arrival he said: 'Whenever I come to London, which is at least four times a year for conferences and the theatre, the first thing I do is go to Berry Brothers at number Three St James Street, Piccadilly, to buy six bottles of good wine and one bottle of superb wine. In my room I have' he continued in low, dark and confidential tones, 'already decanted by room service one hour before my expected return, a bottle of 1955 Chateau Margaux. Thirty years old, brown in colour and with an immense aroma of age and wisdom and utter, utter confidence. Will you' he asked as though it was the last dance and he had finally plucked up courage, 'will you join me if I promise, hand on heart, to behave and advance you nothing but the story of my life?'

Fearing and hoping he would break his promise I accepted. We drank this wine-from-another-planet and he told me that he was researching – wait for it – 'chaos'.

'Chaos' he revealed to me, 'is the new discipline raging through and binding together all the disciplines of science which' he informed me, 'during the last half century have been peeling away from one another into specialist corners.'

Did you know, sisters, that all is chaos in the physical world out there?

'Far from discovering a law and order to all things as Newton predicted, nothing' he was rivetingly dramatic about it, 'nothing happens in quite the same way twice. We are victims of' and here he introduced me to one of the most tenderly formulated notions I've ever heard so harken to it, sisters, 'we are victims of "the sensitive dependence on initial conditions"'. I'll repeat it for verily is it lovely: 'the sensitive dependence on initial conditions, a phenomenon known as: "the butterfly effect" which is' he informed me, 'the notion that a butterfly stirring the air today in Peking can transform storm systems next month in New York. You hit a storm, you can feel it, but who will ever know which butterfly was where that caused it? Chaos!' he warned me, 'all is chaos.'

And when he asked me what *I* did I found myself weeping as I described how my husband had nagged me for years to found a business of vintage Christmas puddings and how I had resisted and he had been right and I became successful and now we lived in what he glorified as his 'divine discontent' but which you, I and all the world knows was blood, tears, and yes, chaos! I had told no one till then. The Chateau Margaux, assisted no doubt by Gustav Mahler, had released my confession and – here's the point – revealed the possibility of reconciliation. But, when I returned home, I discovered – he'd fled. Yes. Fled! Men don't leave, they flee – guilt in their hearts, terror and chaos up their arse.

Beware of the red sauce, sisters, it's hot!

SCENE ELEVEN

MONTCRIEFF's study.

He's typing a sentence.

MONTCRIEFF: 'The great attribute of chaos is that you can count on it! Chaos is dependable…'

(Calling.) Is that *your* experience of life, my once-upon-a-time princess? That chaos is dependable?

> *Listens as though to her reply which gives him pleasure.*

There's no chaos in *you*, is there? In you is the still centre all men crave. How fortunate I am to have found you. And I warn you I will keep you all to myself, tucked away in these hills, chaotic old humanity left far behind…

My ex-darling was an archdeacon of chaos. Not her Christmas-pudding affairs, oh no! Those were kept in order. Her emotional affairs! Those! The chaos lay in her emotions. Her heart produced a turbulence the unpredictability of which had me and she and she and me buffeted around our lives like helpless flotsam in a gale.

Oh she told me about him, her physics professor. She couldn't resist letting me know every pass made after I left. One conversation with him about the new science of chaos and she knew all about it. She's the kind who attends a lecture on a complex subject and overnight is an instant expert! That was she. What I called 'a topper'! Any item of knowledge you presumed to offer a company, she could top it.

'I see the Prime Minister has accepted an invitation to the Middle East.'

'Ah, but have you heard his wife has refused to accompany him in protest against their treatment of women?'

'They've reached the moon then!'

'Yes. Took them twenty-seven hours and forty-three point two minutes'.

'I hear What's-his-name is going to star in Thingamebob's new movie.'

'Well that was the plan, dear, had their plane not crashed half an hour ago!'

I don't know where she got her information from.
Her nipples seemed to act like antennae to the world's airwaves.

But I really didn't mind her knowing things. *That* wasn't our problem.

SCENE TWELVE

MISCHA's apartment.

A pause in their main course.

MINERVA: When I first saw him, I mean 'saw' him, you know what I mean – SAW! I thought – now – *that's* small. I thought that's probably the smallest I'd *ever* seen. Little! In fact it looked to me like it was growing inwards – in fear maybe, desperately trying to crawl back to wherever it came from. And I'd been waiting for this moment for a long time. Years! We'd been admirers for five years, contemplating each other from afar – until – this moment arrived. And I looked down and I thought: *this* is what you've been waiting for? All these years – *this*? I mean a stud he could never have been, except the kind that holds a collar in place, maybe. And when I told him –

MISCHA: You *told* him?

MINERVA: Of course I told him. No secrets if you want good lovemaking. And when I told him, he blanched, as though I'd told him in a roomful of friends.

MISCHA: Surprise, surprise!

MINERVA: But I mollified him. 'No malt during the war, huh?'

CLAIRE: They care about size, don't they? It really matters to them. No understanding of a woman's needs. Thick pricks and thick heads!

MISCHA: *(Shocked.)* Claire!

CLAIRE: We're here to talk about men, aren't we? 'Let's have an orgy of food, wine and derision,' Minerva said to me.

MISCHA: She didn't say it to me.

CLAIRE: You're so prudish about sex.

MISCHA: Not about sex but about –

CLAIRE: What? About what?

MISCHA: A certain respect. For the privacy of life.

CLAIRE: I don't think anything should be private.

MISCHA: That's an outrageous thing to say.

CLAIRE: Why? Literature is full of revealed private moments. That's what we turn to literature for – to pry into other lives.

MISCHA: That's not what *I* read literature for.

CLAIRE: And for what then *do* you read literature?

MISCHA: Illumination.

CLAIRE: The more intimate and private, the more illuminating!

MISCHA: About emotional pain, yes. Not physical deficiencies.

CLAIRE: Why?

MISCHA: Physical deficiencies make us vulnerable.

CLAIRE: And emotional ones don't?

MISCHA: Not in the same way.

CLAIRE: Explain!

MISCHA: Physical deficiencies invite derision, emotional ones invite pity.

CLAIRE: In the love and war of life, pity and derision are inevitable companions.

MINERVA: Well you two are an exciting match. It's like tennis.

MISCHA: You *would* reduce life to a tennis tournament.

MINERVA: Don't get at *me*!

CLAIRE: Do you feel guilty for leaving Leo, Mischa?

MISCHA: No. I might have felt guilty if *he'd* have left *me*. I'd have feared I'd driven him away.

CLAIRE: Is she trying to tell us something?

MINERVA: I think I'll reheat the oil.

SCENE THIRTEEN

MONTCRIEFF's study.

MONTCRIEFF: Our problem was me: I had broody longings for immortality. Babies and literature – she stood it for twenty-five years then kicked me out. And who can blame her? Babies and literature. Lit-er-a-ture!

And what is it? Scavenging! A writer is a vulture that picks at the dead and the partly living. Well, not quite. But who can deny the element of scavenging in literature? Hovering over the livers and lovers, the mad and the dying, recording their passions, picking up their mistakes, weaving patterns out of their laughter and lunacy. All my

best lines are other people's, Oscar, and I make my living
from him and her and a soup-çon of imagination the
trick of which you can buy at any academic supermarket.
Writer? Huh! I'm a picker-up, a pecker-off, a nibbler of
this and that from here and there, an intellectual magpie,
an emotional thief, a beachcomber of other people's lives.
And when I've got it all down in a book I go in to a market
place and I take it out of my pocket like a vendor of dirty
postcards, slightly ashamed. 'You buy? Cheap and lovely
literature! Best art in town! Here, in my pocket! Ssh! Don't
answer too loud. No one else must see and hear.'

You think I exaggerate, dearly beloved, my darling, my
dove, my heart? Although there's nothing wrong with a
little bit of exaggeration, I promise you I do not.

So what could she expect me to do with love, my ex, my
producer-of-vintage-Christmas-puddings-out-of-which-she-
has-made-a-small-fortune? What is love but another sack of
discarded expectations to be sorted out, selected, listed and
filed for lit-er-a-ture?

> *Picks up and reads from one of the letters he's been
> folding into envelopes.*

(Reading.) 'Dear Jason, my new novel is about chaos…
in the past…you have published…but now I think…
something new, something special…would you read…?'

> *Pauses to consider what he's written, sardonic and
> resigned.*

Archivists, that's all we are, of other people's fond
eccentricities, tragic errors, their lost illusions. Literature!
Lit-er-a-ture! LIT. ER. A. TURE!

Are you still with me, my honey, my heart?

SCENE FOURTEEN

MISCHA's apartment.

MINERVA: In the last years he began talking to himself. Lived in his head. His ideal women lived in his head never the real world.

MISCHA: Do you think we can really be honest about men?

MINERVA: About them or with them?

MISCHA: With them, about them, either.

MINERVA: Well, I was honest *with* them. Credited the bastard with my business success; told him I loved him but that he was a bastard; confessed to a fantasy about making love to a stranger...

MISCHA: Claire? *(No response.)* Claire you don't seem really to be here? Are you sure you don't want to watch Vincent being interviewed?

> *CLAIRE abruptly deflects the question. What follows is a moment of coming together.*

CLAIRE: Which of you wooed?

MINERVA: Wooed?

CLAIRE: Wooed! Wooed! I woo, he woos, she woos, they wooed...

MINERVA: *(Sings.)* 'And we'll all woo together...' Yes! I've wooed, dammit! I've stood at the barricades of feminism and roared my fury at frivolous men and their infantile ways and yet –

CLAIRE: – and yet, admit! You have wooed like a slave.

MINERVA: Like a slave!

MISCHA: 'Come live with me' you said to him, 'and I will be your factotum...'

MINERVA: Yes!

CLAIRE: 'Scream for me to scratch your back and I'll come running…'

MINERVA: Yes, yes!

MISCHA: 'I will be near you but not under your feet, I will comfort but not suffocate you, I will wait until you can bear no longer *not* to touch me!'

MINERVA: I promised! I pleaded!

CLAIRE: 'Of course I must work but – this will I do and that will I do…'

MISCHA: You plotted your seductions, planned your passions…

CLAIRE: Days of scheming, dreaming, gentle words and promises…

MINERVA: True! True! I even promised to change my fucking politics for them – all true! As soon as I found a man I wanted – into action! Instinctively! My whole being! Despite everything! I wanted to cook for him, iron his shirts, pour him drinks, cut interesting articles out of newspapers. I found a different hairstyle, tried new perfumes, new make-up. I bought new dresses to delight him, incredible nightdresses to entice him. I even went back to lacy, silk underwear and suspenders and re-discovered my pleasure in them. I was amazed and shocked how easily it all came back to me. I wanted – God damn it – I wanted to look after him!

> *Silence.*

MISCHA: We all want to look after him.

CLAIRE: Speak for yourself. I want to be looked after. I want to be guarded against cruelty and stupidity, protected from dirty minds and ugly souls.

> *CLAIRE makes a sudden movement and knocks over a glass.*

MISCHA: I'm worried about you.

CLAIRE: Well don't be!

SCENE FIFTEEN

TV studio. VINCENT being interviewed.

VINCENT: I'm glad you've asked me that question. But I'd
better warn you my reply will be controversial. Few
people know *how* to behave as equals. They either want to
dominate or be subservient. It's a fraught problem, central
to relationships between priests and their flock, politicians
and their adherents, capital and labour, men and men,
women and women, men and women!

Equality is a Queenly concept we all love to love because
it flatters us. But she's not an easy lady to comprehend.
Consider: if you place a simple mind alongside a wise
mind and declare them equal in the sight of God you will
at once intimidate the simple mind. It can't compete. If you
place an *aggressively* simple mind alongside a wise mind that
is totally *without* aggression, and declare *them* equal then
you at once intimidate the wise mind. The one can't handle
wisdom, the other can't handle belligerence.

Look at the problems between men and women – and I
think we should because I believe the 21st century will
be the century of the woman – though not without a kind
of emotional bloodshed. Most women – and many are
not going to like what I say, and I may be losing myself
their votes but not too many I hope because I'd like to
think I appeal to those who vote for honesty rather than
demagogy – but most women seem not to *want* to behave
as equals! They either want to dominate or serve. There
may be historical or social reasons for this, but I'm not a
sociologist, I can only describe my experience of those
relationships.

We are here dealing with an uncomfortable concept. Most men and women in their relationships do not eye one another as potential partners but as potential combatants. The question they present to themselves is not 'do I love?' but 'can I win?'

SCENE SIXTEEN

MISCHA's apartment.

They have finished second course.

MINERVA: Was that good or was not that good?

MISCHA: It was very good.

CLAIRE: It was like nothing I've ever tasted before.

MINERVA: Let's not go over the top. Praise, I enjoy. Adulation is suspect.

CLAIRE: No! I mean it. I'm serious about food. I've had lots of fondues and the sauces offered nearly always taste like each other. With these I had the feeling that each cube of meat came from a different cow. A cube of meat dipped in the avocado sauce seemed to come from Switzerland. The cube dipped in the yellow sauce was undoubtedly a cow from the Argentine. The cube dipped in the red hot sauce – don't expect any of this to be logical – although it was hot, was unmistakably a cow from England.

MINERVA: An English cow – curried?

CLAIRE: Just so.

MINERVA: I love that you've distinguished tastes in my food, sister dear, but sense you do not make.

CLAIRE: Don't *say* that! That's what *he* kept telling me: 'you do not make sense.' How I hate that sentence. *(Mimicking.)* 'Forgive me saying it but you do not make sense, my dear.' It was important to him to keep me just a few rungs lower.

MINERVA: I thought he was a generous spirited man your Vincent.

CLAIRE: He was, he was! Generous, able, dynamic company – an adequate lover too, but he was – oh, that special brand of put-downer. There I was – high on being the researcher and mistress of a shadow cabinet minister but – not a week went by that he didn't talk about the brilliant, erudite talented women of the past – George Elliot, Beatrice Webb, Virginia Woolf –

MISCHA: – Jane Austen, the Brontes, Mary Shelley –

> *A subtle change of tone emerges. A list that began as a whip of the past turns into a panegyric roll of honour – another moment of coming together.*

MINERVA: Boadicea, Elizabeth I, Catherine the Great –

MISCHA: Georges Sand, Rosa Luxembourg, Simone de Beauvoir –

MINERVA: What about Heloise, Beatrice, and Eve – who got us out of boring old paradise?

CLAIRE: Right! A marvellous heritage of women. But Vincent beat me with them, the greats of the past, as though he himself was one of those very greats. And he constantly laid upon me facts he knew I'd not be able to contradict. He didn't do it maliciously, oppressively, there was no spite in the man but – I don't know. It was as though he didn't know how to behave as an equal. He *talked* about equality, talked like one who *believed* himself your equal. But he seemed incapable of *behaving* like one. Perhaps I *wasn't* his equal – he was after all a very capable man: astute at political assessment, shrewd at human assessment, quick-witted, good memory, widely read, social graces and – something I admired in him more than anything else – intellectual courage, he took risks in his career, but – it was essential to his self-confidence that someone was around twenty four hours a day to reassure him that he was superior, not by word but simply by *being*. I was that being. With me he could be benign, generous, modest, helpful, over-flowing with advice. I made him seem wise to himself, allowed him to bestow bounty, permitted his magnanimity to blossom.

Her tone changes.

CLAIRE: And I loved every minute of it.

MISCHA: That's awful, Claire. That's shocking and degrading.

CLAIRE: Ah, moral Mischa who imagines she's found her knight in shining armour, her prince Charming. Do you really think me shocking and degraded? Performing the service of making him appear wise and superior had the reverse effect of making *me* feel wise and superior. Permitting him to assume control simply meant *I* was in control. Do you think I *really* considered him wiser than me? As the servant who deferred, as his admirer who bowed I was able to manipulate him for my own needs.

MINERVA: I think my Chateau Margaux '55 has got to her.

CLAIRE: And do you think I *loved* him? that I even like men as a species? I – have needs, they – provide. They fuck my appetites away and I can command high salaries.

MISCHA: The lady doth protest too much, methinks.

CLAIRE: For that I must dissemble a state of mind that allows them to imagine *they* are in control. But oh are they not! And *you* know they're not. Between ourselves let's be honest: men are for manipulating.

MINERVA: I'd drink to that if I had any more Chateau Margaux '55.

CLAIRE: Why else were we given tears?

MINERVA: I can open a bottle of lesser wine?

CLAIRE drives on.

MISCHA is watching her closely.

CLAIRE: And sighs and soft curves?

MINERVA: I think I *will* open a bottle of lesser wine. *(Does so.)*

CLAIRE: And what about eyes? What *can't* be put into eyes, tell
me? Like bottles you can fill at will with different colours,
so with our eyes – vessels to be filled with all those glorious
shades of emotion. Gaiety one minute, vulnerability
the next. A touch of melancholy here, a hint of longing
there, the wicked brilliance of passion, the damp ducts
of helplessness, the milky hue of modesty – whatsoever
emotion is required for our ends we can call up into our
eyes, and few men can resist.

And let us not, sisters, let us not talk about our sexuality.
That would be giving too much away, wouldn't it? You,
Mischa, ask can we be honest about men? You, Minerva,
say there'll be no pussy-footing around this table?
Right! Recall the moments, those splendid moments
of total control, when you've stood naked and become
triumphantly aware of the power in each moulded part –

MINERVA: Who on earth is she talking about?

CLAIRE: – when you've isolated each magnetic mound and
known its sensuous weight in gold.

MINERVA: She's not talking about me.

CLAIRE: There you've stood, knowing the allure of breasts
drew hands. There you've stood, knowing that mound at
the base of your belly drew hands. And that belly – oh I
knew what drew my teenage lover to stroke and circle the
palm of his hand round and round and round and round.

MINERVA: Nine out of ten women would not recognise
themselves in any of that.

CLAIRE: Would not admit it! But – for most women there was
at least one time in their lives when they stood before a
mirror facing their flesh and aware that every voluptuous

part was bewitching, delicious, magnetic! The curve of a
neck, the long soft side of their arms, the down of a thigh,
hips to be held, buttocks to be squeezed, fingers and toes
and nipples to be sucked. Power! Pulsating, intoxicated,
confident, through every nerve-end – power! The tool
we must learn to handle for delight and the security of
our lives – power! The power to bestow that one deep
and excruciating pleasure that all men helplessly crave
– it's ours! And with it we have them, malleable, for
manipulating – men! Deny it if you dare, sisters dear!
Contradict me if you dare, sisters dear! Talk to me of love if
you dare, dear, dear sisters, dear!

MINERVA: I think it's time you presented us with your dessert,
Claire.

End of Act One.

Act Two

SCENE ONE

The garden.

LEO – his lawnmower – three more attempts. Fails. Sits.

LEO: The universe is a ball
    bounced by a child
    living on a planet
    placed in a universe bounced
    by a child
    living on a planet
    placed in a universe bounced
    by a child...

> *It is his private incantation, his secular rosary. But it is not really what is preoccupying him.*

> *Slowly, working it out, almost word by word...*

The real difference between men and women is that women have the perceptive power to *recognise* paradise when they see it, the emotional capacity to *hang* onto it, and the confidence not to care whether paradise wants them or not. Men are never certain it's *paradise* they see. That's why she stopped loving me – she'd seen paradise. A man who she knew, without the slightest, the merest, the merest, the slightest hesitation – she was in love with. And in she zoomed.

'You' she said, 'do not support me either emotionally, intellectually, or in bed. You suffer from' she said, 'constipation of the imagination.'

And she was right! I was dead! I only came alive in business conferences. What was wrong with me, was me!

What could I do? Stopped loving me! Ceased! Dried up! Unloved any longer. I had become – unlovable!

SCENE TWO

MISCHA's apartment.

CLAIRE has calmed down. Contrite almost, shocked for having gone too far.

The others are waiting on her.

CLAIRE: Something light. A cheesecake. A lot of calories – I know – but – light. Fluffy.

Long pause.

MISCHA: And the dessert wine?

CLAIRE: Tokay. From Hungary.

MISCHA: Three or four star?

CLAIRE: Four.

MISCHA whistles in admiration.

Another long pause.

MINERVA: No more? That's it?

MISCHA: When did you first eat it?

Even longer pause.

MINERVA: Well?

CLAIRE: *(Finally.)* In Auschwitz.

MINERVA: God help us!

MISCHA: *(Understanding.)* Another parliamentary excursion no doubt.

CLAIRE: Yes.

MISCHA: Polish members of parliament invite British members of parliament to visit rebuilt Warsaw, beautiful

Cracow, the ski slopes of Zakopane, and Auschwitz – obligatory.

CLAIRE: I didn't want to go. I hate confrontation with suffering, feeling helpless, weeping tears I haven't earned.

Pause.

MINERVA: So?

CLAIRE: I held back.

MINERVA: And?

CLAIRE: Returned to the gate.

MINERVA: Where you were fed cheesecake? *(No response.)* Jesus! It's like getting blood out of a stone.

CLAIRE: I saw a grey-haired old woman staring at me. She held a plastic carrier bag in her hand which made me think she was a local. I nodded to her, and she spoke to me. It was quite a shock, actually. She had a heavy Polish accent tucked inside a heavy American one.

'You're not going to *visit* are you!' she said. She didn't ask, she stated. She seemed to know. 'I see many like you' she said. 'They come to the gates but they can't go on. I don't blame them. *I* only come' she said, 'because my family is here, and if my family wasn't here *I* wouldn't come either.'

And she told me this story of how her entire family – parents, brothers, sisters, uncles, aunts, cousins and grandparents – all! Gassed! She survived because she was the clever one and the family saved up money to send her to study in Paris. And it seems her youngest sister, in the midst of all that deprivation, used to save crumbs to feed a baby bird she'd found.

'So I come every year to feed birds and visit my family'.

MISCHA: And *that* made you weep!

CLAIRE: Aren't you the clever one!

MISCHA: Not merely for her sister – the bird lover, but also for Environment Shadow Minister Vincent Ferguson, your own lover, and for the helplessness of that and most other things in life.

CLAIRE: The really clever one.

MISCHA: One event may prompt it but every tear is finally for everything.

CLAIRE: And to console me this grey-haired old woman fed me her home-made cheesecake. 'Here' she said. 'It's my own recipe. And I've given it a name.' I asked her what name? 'Five-thousand-years-of-suffering-cheesecake' she replied. Which made me laugh. We both laughed. Imagine – feeding birds, eating cheesecake and laughing at the gates of Auschwitz!

Silence.

MISCHA: *'We have a little sister, and she hath no breasts: what shall we do for our sister in the day when she shall be spoken for?'*

Silence.

MINERVA: Feel like telling the Puzaltski story?

CLAIRE: At this moment I think – no!

SCENE THREE

MONTCRIEFF in his study.

MONTCRIEFF: Travel! The one thing you and I are going to do is travel. When I think of all the exotic places I haven't seen I get into a panic. The Valois of France, the rain forests of Brazil, the back streets of Cairo, the deserts of Arabia, the Temples of Thailand – panic! When I think of all the *books* I haven't read – panic! The tastes, the experiences, the challenges – panic!

Pause, as though listening.

Of course I get seasick! Seasick, carsick, bus-sick, people-sick. You name it, I get sick of it.

Pause, as though listening.

What makes you think I'm a misanthropist? I'm just growing old, and growing old is the process whereby contempt for most humankind is confirmed.

Thinks sadly about this. Recovers.

But never mind, we'll take the car on the ferry, risk drowning, and I'll dance you through the Europe of my wild youth. Down and Out in Paris, The First Film Festival in Cannes, The Prague Spring, The Vienna Waltz, The Miracle in Milan ... Isn't that what you're supposed to do with a young mistress? Take her back over your youth? Vivid times, my darling. B.C.

Pause

Before Cynicism.

Pause

You're not really there, are you? I imagine you –

Pause, trying –

– invent you –

Pause, trying –

– *will* you into existence –

Pause. Finally, with a hint of sad

envy –

But whoever you are *you* will always be the one who gives birth, won't you ...?

SCENE FOUR

MISCHA's apartment.

All in their own way are a little tipsy.

MISCHA: I used to play this game with Leo, drive him mad.

'What' I'd badger him, 'what one, unexpected thing would you like to do in your life? You're a financial analyst' I'd taunt him, 'for a big, big, big stock broking firm. But what – what is the one secret thing you've really, really, really always wanted to do?'

MINERVA: What'd he say?

MISCHA: Didn't! Couldn't!

MINERVA: Wouldn't, p'raps?

MISCHA: No! Couldn't! Constipation of the imagination! A genuinely sweet, genuinely kind man who genuinely comprehended nothing in the world except money. Machines, children, paintings, music, literature – all genuinely bewildered him. Had no meaning for him. What's the point of a child – it doesn't converse or produce? What's the point of a machine if it doesn't operate at a touch? What's the point of a painting – people and the world are there in front of you…? Even his own 'thing' bewildered him.

MINERVA: 'Thing'? 'Thing'? It's got a name. William! Willie for short.

CLAIRE: A marauder!

MISCHA: A shlong!

MINERVA: A totem-pole!

CLAIRE: *(Mock macho.)* 'Don't be frightened but here – are my credentials!'

MINERVA: *(Mock American macho, hand on imaginary zip.)* 'Are you sure you can handle this?'

> *MISCHA stands, legs astride, looking down.*

MISCHA: Bewildered him! It was his stranger-in-paradise! He'd gyrate *(She does so.)* watching it loll about. 'My sleepy lion' he used to call it. It was the funniest thing he ever said. 'Look at my sleepy lion ha ha!'

MINERVA: Whatever was Leo's attraction for God's sake?

MISCHA: *(Giggling.)* His 'sleepy lion' I think.

MINERVA: She's off! I told you, dearly beloved, we'd gather to talk about men.

MISCHA: It was enormous! It used to hang between his legs and he'd stare down at it in genuine bewilderment, didn't seem to know what else it was for other than you-know-what.

> *She's still there, staring down, herself a little unsteady.*

Stare, waiting! Hoping something would happen by osmosis. He never quite made the connection between 'it' and the sexual act. I tried undressing slowly, slinkily, to help. No use! I'd finally have to man-handle it the way one slaps dough around the table.

MINERVA: Ouch!

MISCHA: When it did finally lumber awake it was, I must confess, rather magnificent. But not for long. Without imagination it soon erupted and then collapsed like a dynamited old Victorian chimney stack. Obsolete!

MINERVA: An obsolete cock! Yes – I'd say that describes most men.

CLAIRE: I think you're very unfair about Leo. He has limitations, who hasn't? He was gauche, his brain didn't live inside his body. But he was witty and generous and did you ever hear him on love?

MISCHA: He talked to *you* about love?

CLAIRE: I didn't love him. He could.

MISCHA: Perhaps he confided in you a secret, unexpected desire?

CLAIRE: Tell us your's, Mischa. What one, unexpected thing would *you* like to do in your life?

MISCHA: Can't say!

CLAIRE: Oh go on. Tell us.

MISCHA: Too shy.

CLAIRE: What, between gals?

MISCHA: Especially between 'gals'.

CLAIRE: Well that makes it immediately intriguing.

MINERVA: You weren't too shy to talk about obsolete cocks.

MISCHA: Tell us your's Minerva. What one unexpected thing would *you* like to do in your life?

MINERVA: Oh mine's easy. I'd like to climb the outside of Big Ben.

Her friends are incredulous.

MISCHA: Whatever for?

CLAIRE: I can't conceive of any more vacuous ambition in life.

MINERVA: That's because you don't suffer from virgo like I do.

CLAIRE: You mean vertigo.

MINERVA: That's what I said, vertigo.

CLAIRE: Do you think we're drunk?

SCENE FIVE

TV Studios.

VINCENT being interviewed.

VINCENT: If I were Prime Minister? I'm not sure that's the
sort of question I should be answering. On the other hand
I long ago decided – and our leader accepted this when
I was invited to take up the post of Shadow Minister
for Environment – that I was not going to tailor my
personality to a political career. My political career would
have to tailor itself to me.

Party policy you'll find in manifestos drawn up by
committee, but a party leader is flesh and blood. A myriad
of idiosyncrasies. Idiosyncratic habits, idiosyncratic
tastes, idiosyncratic thoughts. Now I'm against the cult
of personality but I can't be bland! I can't fade into an
anonymous background.

So, if I were Prime Minister I'd want the people to be
in no uncertainty as to the kind of person I am. They
should know what I think, believe, fear and even doubt.
Especially my doubts. I mean – there are a lot of very
important issues to be considered: the eternal cycle of
injustice, revolution, injustice, revolution … for example;
the relationship of education to liberty; the role of envy in
human conflict. It's not enough for a leader of a party to be
good at putting pennies on a tax here and taking them off
there – what's the quality of *thought* behind the decision,
that's what *I'd* want to know.

So, if I were Prime Minister I'd set up a chain of key
lectures. Say four a year. And my priority themes would
be: The Individual Spirit – does capitalism release
or shackle it? Second: Human Nature – good, evil or
irrational. Third: The Decline of Language and its
Relationship to Inhumanity. Fourth: Violence to Achieve
Ends – the vicious circle.

> *His last words fade away with the cross-fading
> lights –*

SCENE SIX

MISCHA's apartment.

The women are slightly tipsier.

MINERVA: What do you look at first when you look at a man?

CLAIRE: His bum!

MINERVA: Only his bum?

MISCHA: Thighs for me.

MINERVA: Bums and thighs. Any advance on bums and thighs?

CLAIRE: His eyes, his eyes, I'm his for his eyes.

MISCHA: Shoulders, shoulders, I'm his for his shoulders.

MINERVA: Lips, lips. Let his tongue lick his lips.

CLAIRE: *(Singing it.)* And let us not forget the bulge.

> *All three find a simple harmony. Another moment of coming together.*

ALL: The bulge! The bulge! And let us not forget the bulge!

> *Laughter.*
>
> *Subsides.*
>
> *Silence.*

MISCHA: *(Entering her own world.)*

I am the rose of Sharon, and the lily of the valleys.

MINERVA: Mischa, Mischa, Mischa. Tell us your secret.

MISCHA: *As the lily among thorns so is my love among the daughters.*

MINERVA: Don't be shy with your sisters who love you. What one unexpected thing would you like to do in your life. Climb a mountain? Cross the Sahara? Live a year with the Bedouins? Or in a nunnery? Would you like to get thee to a nunnery – which as we all know was Hamlet's inspired suggestion for the woman he loved?

MISCHA: *Stay me with flagons, comfort me with apples, for I am sick of love.*

CLAIRE: Oh wise, mysterious Mischa, who knows what we think before we have thought it, who will take her secrets to the grave.

>*Something in this draws MISCHA's attention to CLAIRE, who turns away.*
>
>*MISCHA let's it pass.*
>
>*Silence, then –*

MISCHA: The truth about paradise is this: the serpent was Jewish!

Leo was obsessed with the thought that paradise lost was the cause of conflict between men and women. Men can't forgive women because Eve seduced Adam into biting the apple which lost them paradise. But he missed the point, my poor Leo. The conflict is not between men and women over the fall from grace, it's between men on one side and women and Jews on the other. 'Get thee with learning' whispered the Jewish serpent. 'Bite! You'll see better!' *He* knew a useful tool when he saw it. So Eve, being a woman with an instinct for the good things in life, and having more courage than her male companion, bit, and got pregnant with learning, and lost paradise! For all of us! *(Pause.)* Been hated ever since. *(Pause.)* Oppressed and hated. *(Pause.)* Jews and women! *(Pause.)* For knowing too much.

I read in the paper the other day that a woman got off for murdering her husband because he beat her, for long periods, cruelly, until she couldn't stand it any longer. And the occasion when he beat her most was when she used a word with more than one syllable. 'Don't you use educated words with me' he cried at her. 'Don't you come the clever stuff with me. Bam! Wallop! Bash! Take that and that and that!' *(Pause.)* Women and Jews. *(Pause.)* For biting an apple. *(Pause.)* Funny old life.

> *The speech came out of the air, and into the air disappears.*

MINERVA: Claire Dawn Hope?

CLAIRE: Yes, Malt? What can I do for you, M.A.L.T.?

MINERVA: Tell us, what one unexpected thing would *you* like to do in your life?

CLAIRE: I? Me? My secret unexpected hidden desire?

MINERVA: I know! Don't tell me! You want to be whipped!

CLAIRE: No! Though I'd quite like to be let loose with a whip on some men I know.

MISCHA: Come, Claire, you don't want to take your secret to the grave do you?

CLAIRE: My secret wish has always been to sing a pop song. Just one. Specially written for me. Rehearse with a group for as long as it takes and then – cut a single! A song I can sing my heart out with, and everyone would dance to! Dance, dance, dance, dance, dance...

> *MISCHA watches her very carefully as she dances.*

SCENE SEVEN

MONTCRIEFF's study.

MONTCRIEFF: Are you one of those young women who complain the world is dominated by men? Well you may be right, you may be right. We're a bullying lot. But here's some questions to ponder. Can men be said to have shaped the world when they're the product of their mothers?

And take the game of chess – a game I rarely play, and when I do I can't think many moves ahead. Consider the queen, her main task is to protect the king and to attack any one who threatens him. She can move where she likes – diagonally, horizontally, back and forth. And here's the question: why do you think the queen was chosen to be aggressive, defensive and free-wheeling, while the king creeps crippled across the board one step at a time?

> *Reaches for TV remote control, flicks screen alive. We hear VINCENT's VOICE.*

VINCENT: I suppose this line of questioning means you're approaching dangerous terrain.

> *MONTCRIEFF wickedly chuckles as he settles to enjoy his viewing.*

SCENE EIGHT

MISCHA's apartment.

She's serving coffee.

MINERVA: The real problem with Monctrieff was that he couldn't face not being Dostoevsky.

MISCHA: Arabic coffee.

MINERVA: 'So what?' I'd yell at him, 'absolutely no one else in the world is Dostoevsky either!'

MISCHA: With cumin seed.

MINERVA: He couldn't have our babies and he wasn't Dostoevsky so he left me.

MISCHA: That simple?

MINERVA: Nothing is that simple.

CLAIRE: And what drew Mischa to her Prince Charming, her knight on a white horse?

MISCHA: Harmony. His head was inside his body.

CLAIRE: Lucky you.

MISCHA: You don't like me anymore do you?

No response.

We were all such good friends.

No response.

I've never hurt you, betrayed you, spoken ill of you behind your back. You can't hold it against me that I suggested Vincent hire you, surely?

Long pause.

You think *I* talked him out of you, don't you?

CLAIRE: Didn't you?

MISCHA: Oh, Claire. I have great faults but I'm not treacherous. He's a family man with a political career. He made a choice.

No response.

I'd also love those days back. Good times. Shared pleasures, laughter, consolations, friendship …

CLAIRE: It's your 'wisdom' I can't bear, your fucking, melancholy Jewish wisdom. Not all those five thousand years of suffering have prevented you from dreaming on and on and on about your Prince Charmings, your knights on white horses, your Messiahs.

MISCHA: *(Bewildered.)* Why should that make you resent me so?

CLAIRE: Because all idealism offends me. There are no knights in shining armour out there. Prince Charmings live in the story books of silly girls. Messiahs never come. Leo was a good man with a sense of humour. Your families came from the same village in Russia. He was on his knees to you most of the time.

MISCHA: I didn't want that.

CLAIRE: He would have been your doormat.

MISCHA: I didn't want that.

CLAIRE: He dressed you, fed you, housed you, and answered your every whim.

MISCHA: I didn't want any of that!

CLAIRE: No! You wanted endless intellectual conversations, endless evenings out to the theatre, endless trips to historical sites and an amazing circle of the endlessly interesting, the endlessly stimulating, the endlessly erudite.

MISCHA: What the hell is wrong with any of that?

MINERVA: What the hell is wrong with any of that is that no man is endlessly interesting for ever and ever and ever amen.

MISCHA: Is any woman?

CLAIRE: Is any *body*?

MISCHA: Bitterness is a cancer, Claire.

CLAIRE: There it is! Fucking melancholy Jewish wisdom again!

SCENE NINE

LEO's garden.

Sitting on a bench. Disconsolate.

LEO: Let us contemplate suicide.

First problem: how? Armoury? I do not possess. A knife in my heart? My hands would be unable to push. Sleeping pills? I would fall asleep before taking enough of them. Gas? She cooked by electricity. My car? Ah! My car! Close garage doors. Sit. Switch on. Breath deeply. A comfortable way to go.

Second problem: why?

Long, long pause.

Third problem: A will. Is my will made out? Of course. Do I want to make changes? None. Are all my affairs in order? All!

> *Pause.*

Return to problem two: why? Everyone is interesting.

> *Pause.*

Even when they're boring they're interesting.

> *Pause.*

Only not for as long as those who are *not* boring.

> *Pause.*

And *I* am definitely boring. I *am* boring! I am *boring!*

If I stop and try to make my mind think something interesting, I can't! Look! I sit here and squeeze and squeeze, like trying to get juice from a shrivelled up old orange and –

> *Hold for a long pause as he tries to fill his mind with something to surprise himself.*

(*cont.*) – I can't! Nothing comes! Only if I think about – my job – my profession. *That* excites me – the flow, the placing, the reproductive mechanisms of money. I can't help it! Money excites me. Why should I be ashamed of that, Mischa? It helped you, your family, our friends.

> *Thinks about this.*

Oh God! I'm so boring I bore myself. It's an illness. I need help, treatment, I need pity. Pity not derision...

MISCHAAAAAAAA!

Hardy. I need Hardy. Must phone Hardy. He doesn't think much of me but he'll help. For old time's sake. I'll phone him now. (*Rises.*) I don't really want to die. I want to be loved. I do, I do. Loved.... Looked after...I'll provide the

money, somebody look after me. There must be a cure for
an affliction like boringness.

> *Pause.*

Is there such a word – 'boringness'?

> *Leaves, calling…*

Hardy, Hardy, Hardy…

SCENE TEN

MISCHA's apartment.

CLAIRE: The Puzaltski story.

> *All funny stories rely upon the teller.*
>
> *We write it but the actress is free to restructure it to
> her own style of telling, like a solo violinist given free
> rein in a cadenza.*

Puzaltski was the fourth reserve of a famous American
football team. So famous that it always had star players,
and poor Puzaltski was never ever in fifteen years called on
field to play a match.

Retirement is upon him. Comes the last Saturday in his
career, he wakes up, sits down to his breakfast of steak and
french fries, and says to his wife –

> *– in a heavy 'Brando Waterfront' accent –*

'Dat's it! Finished! I'm not going to der match!'
His wife is aghast.
'You're not going to the match? The last match! It's
unprofessional not to play the last match!'
'Don't tell me!' cries a deeply unhappy and humiliated
Puzaltski. 'But for fifteen years I've been fourth reserve and
I aint never ever been called to play a game. Fifteen years
sitting on der side-lines. Do you have any idea what it's like
only ever to sit on der side-lines and never be a player?
What kindda life was dat?'

'Maybe today' says his wife, 'today they'll call you!'
'Dey haven't called me in fifteen years, why should dey call me on my very last day wid der team?'

His wife is fearful.
'You skip the last match they'll cut off your retirement pension and then where will we be?'
'I'm not going and dey won't cut off my retirement pension and we'll be OK.' Puzaltski is adamant.
'*I'll* go!' cries his distraught wife. 'I'll *take* your place!'
'You?' laughs her husband. 'You're a woman!'

Mrs Puzaltski ignores him.
'I'll get to the locker room early, I'll get into all that gear – who'll know?'
'It won't work.'
'It'll work! I'll just be a number sitting on the side-lines and I won't say a word. Did anybody ever talk to *you*?'
'Never!'
'So – it'll work!'

And away she goes. Locker room. Changes. The coach puts his arm round her and pats her on the bum. Sits on the side-lines. First half of the match, as always, the team remains intact. Then, second half – chaos takes over! Down goes one player. The first reserve is called. Down goes a second payer. The second reserve is called. A very nervous Mrs Puzaltski is sitting on the side-lines.

> *CLAIRE begins to titter.*

(Carefully.) It is a game she does not know how to play!

> *As the story progresses all the women will gradually be drawn in to infectious laughter even before the punch line.*

Fifteen minutes before the end of the game the home team is losing, the fans are not very happy. Then, the unimaginable happens. A third player goes down and the cry goes up for the fourth reserve. 'PUZALTSKI!'

There's no way out. She has to go onto the field.

CLAIRE enacts it.

There she is, bending down, looking around, understanding nothing, praying she'll be called upon to do nothing, and the numbers come. Out of sequence. Meaningless. Fast. Nine! Seven! Three! Five! Two! Wham! She suddenly finds the ball coming her way. She catches! She runs! Of course she doesn't know what *should* be done so she does the right thing in the wrong way. A crazy dash. While she runs with the ball the players jump on each other. Touch down! The fans go wild.

Who is this guy? They've never seen him before. The name is whispered. The whisper spreads and soon the name is on everyone's lips.

'Puzaltski! Puzaltski!'

Meanwhile Mrs Puzaltski is a very bewildered and frightened woman.

'This is not' she says to herself, head bent down, 'a very wise thing to have done.'

The crazy numbers begin again. Different ones. Two! Nine! Seven! One! Ten! She understands nothing, but there again – wham! The ball's in her hands. She runs. Unorthodox. Another touch down! The field's in confusion. The fans are delirious. They're chanting:

PU-ZALT-SKI! PU-ZALT-SKI! PU-ZALT-SKI!

Meanwhile the other side are getting very, very worried indeed, and they get into a huddle.

'I don't know what the fuck's happening' says their captain, 'but one thing's for certain – we gotta nail that guy they call Puzaltski!'

So there they are again. Heads down, numbers flying, and every eye of the enemy team on Mrs Puzaltski who by this time is beginning to enjoy herself. Five! Three! Seven! Two! Eight! Wham! The ball's in her hands again and in a flash eleven men are on top of her. She's out! Cold!

Next thing she knows she's in the dressing room, stripped, and the trainer is over her pushing down at her breasts as though trying to get them to be somewhere else. She opens her eyes and it's obvious – she is amazed! The trainer bends over her full of admiration and reassurance and he says:

'Ya did good Puzaltski, ya did real swell. And don't worry about a ting. I'll have ya right in no time. As soon as I getcha balls back into place your prick will come out of hiding!'

They are convulsed.

SCENE ELEVEN

The last scene will be played as a duet between two settings:

MONTCRIEFF's study followed by MISCHA's apartment.

First: MONTCRIEFF's study.

The phone rings – a ringing which will continue until the laughter has died away and the scene settles.

MONTCRIEFF answers. It is LEO who we hear as 'voiceover'.

At the same time the TV set is on and we can see VINCENT in the last stages of his interview.

His voice will fade in and out but will always be there in the background.

Thus the three men (one actor) perform a 'trio'.

LEO: Hardy? It's Leo, don't hang-up.

MONTCRIEFF: Why should I hang up?

LEO: I know you don't like me but I've always rather
respected you and I need to talk to someone. Someone
who knew Mischa and me well.

MONTCRIEFF: Can I ring you back? Vincent's being
interviewed. He should be writhing on the floor any
minute now.

LEO: *I'll* ring back.

MONTCRIEFF: Why aren't you watching? Once-upon-a-time
friends and all that.

LEO: I'm sorry to have disturbed you.

MONTCRIEFF: They've allowed him to be clever and urbane
but now come the personal questions, and I can't wait to
see what they've found.

LEO: It's important, Hardy. Life or death I'd say.

MONTCRIEFF: Death? You? *You*, Leo?

> *But he's also listening to VINCENT whose voice from
> the screen is louder.*

VINCENT: *(On screen.)* Well it depends how far back you want
to dig into my past, but I don't think there's anything
I need be *too* worried about. Some apple-stealing from
neighbours, a little cheating at school once, truant – that
sort of misdemeanour. I mean I don't imagine you're going
to ask me how my wife and I make love –

> *Nervous laughter.*

MONTCRIEFF: Leo, I don't really think we should be talking
about this over the phone.

LEO: Hardy – would you ask her to come home?

MONTCRIEFF: Let her go, Leo. She's still in love with you-
know-who. Accept it. Now put the phone down, switch on
the TV and watch with bated breath.

LEO: Did you know that our universe is a ball
    bounced by a child
    living on a planet
    placed in a universe bounced
    by a child
    living on a planet...

MONTCRIEFF: LEO!?

Fade in MISCHA's apartment.

MINERVA: Mischa! We still don't know which one, unexpected thing Mischa would like to do in her life. Claire wants to cut a disc, I want to climb a tower – what about you?

MISCHA: You want to know? Striptease!

MINERVA: *(Amazed.)* Striptease?

MISCHA: The one secret, unexpected thing I'd like to do in my life is a striptease.

MINERVA: The woman shocked by Claire's power-of-the-body theory wants to put her body to the test of power?

CLAIRE: She's lying.

MISCHA: I'm secure in my intellect, why should I be lying?

CLAIRE: She wants to be interesting.

MISCHA: In a really, raunchy working-men's club where there is absolutely no brain at work, where the senses are uncontaminated by intellect, where the response is one hundred per cent pure contact between my body and what it makes a man feel, and where, incidentally, I could test Claire's power-of-the-body theory.

MINERVA: I understand my friends not.

CLAIRE: *(Disproportionately angry.)* She's mocking me.

Which makes MISCHA wonder at her even more.

MINERVA: Maybe I was wrong, maybe you *need* to watch Vincent being interviewed.

MONTCRIEFF's study.

LEO: Believe me! Women recognise paradise but men are never certain it's paradise they see.

MONTCRIEFF: Wrong! It's just that women are satisfied with *less* of paradise. Men want it all!

LEO: God! You're clever, Hardy. That's why you can be immune to feminine taunts.

MONTCRIEFF: Me? Immune to feminine taunts?

VINCENT from the screen.

VINCENT: Yes, I had lots of girl-friends before I was married. In my degree course studying politics and economics were some of the most interesting female minds in our generation. For me there's nothing more sexy than an original mind.

MISCHA's apartment.

MINERVA: Claire? Vincent? The interview?

CLAIRE: No.

MINERVA: But they're coming to the decimating part and they're bound to dig up something you didn't know.

CLAIRE: I do not want to see his face, hear his voice, share his thoughts-for-the-day, or know anything about his life whatsoever.

MISCHA: The lady doth protest too much, methinks.

MINERVA: The lady she hath drunk too much, methinks.

CLAIRE: And methinks you're both getting on my tits. *(To MINERVA.)* You're the one who's consumed with hatred of men.

MINERVA: Let's not exaggerate.

CLAIRE: I was just a married man's whore – period!

MISCHA: Oh come on, Claire, he didn't pay you.

CLAIRE: Not in cash but in kind, the good life, the good, good life – the rich, exhilarating, endlessly interesting good life.

MINERVA: There comes that ever hopeful 'endlessly' again.

MISCHA: She always did have a weakness for self-dramatisation.

CLAIRE: Oh, did I now, Mischa the wise, Mischa the pure, Mischa the intellectual of us all? There's nothing you've done wrong in your life is there? Nothing really, really, really reprehensible. All sweetness and light!

> *VINCENT on screen.*

VINCENT: *(In fury.) That* is innuendo! That shouldn't even have been posed as a question. There was absolutely nothing beyond a professional relationship between Claire Dawn Hope and myself and I will take you and your muckraking television company through every court in the land to prove it.

> *Pause. Listening.*

What? That cannot be true...I don't believe...she could not possibly have...

> *MISCHA is looking intently at a miserable, distracted CLAIRE.*
>
> *The dialogue swings between the two settings.*

MISCHA: *(To CLAIRE.)* You told them, didn't you?

MINERVA: You told them?

MONTCRIEFF: *(Incredulous.)* She told them.

LEO: Hardy, are you listening to me?

MONTCRIEFF: *(To LEO on phone.)* Yes, of course she played that game with me.

MISCHA: Damn you, Claire!

MONTCRIEFF: And you know the one secret unexpected thing I'd like to have done in *my* life?

MINERVA: *(Dawning approval.)* She told them.

MONTCRIEFF: Given birth! .

MISCHA: That television researcher who came to ask about Vincent's interests –

MONTCRIEFF: Yes, of course to a child, what else?

MISCHA: – you listed *all* of them, didn't you?

MONTCRIEFF: Penis envy? Nonsense! They can have mine!

MISCHA: Didn't you?

MONTCRIEFF: More trouble than it's worth.

MISCHA: You listed *all* his interests…

MONTCRIEFF: Swap it for a womb any time!

MISCHA: …language, ceramics, stone gardens and Claire Dawn Hope.

MONTCRIEFF: My one envy of women is that they can give birth.

MISCHA: She promised silence but betrayed him.

MINERVA: Do I condone or do I not condone? that is the question.

MONTCRIEFF: Pain? Pain? What pain?

MISCHA: How can you condone? She's destroyed a life.

MONTCRIEFF: Women always want to exclude you.

MISCHA: She promised the affair would remain just between our three couples but she revenged herself.

MINERVA: Revenge has an honourable history.

MISCHA: Revenge has a primitive history.

MONTCRIEFF: Breast-feeding, staying up all night with it....

MISCHA: And with her revenge she betrayed us, too.

MINERVA: Betrayed?

MISCHA: Yes, betrayed.

MONTCRIEFF: 'You'll never understand' they say, 'I had the pain you had the pleasure.'

MINERVA: God! You're self-righteous, Mischa.

MONTCRIEFF: I'd take *all* the pain for that miracle of birth.

MISCHA: *You* see self-righteous, I see outrage!

> *MISCHA, simultaneously with MONTCRIEFF's last speech, hurls words at CLAIRE underneath him.*

MONTCRIEFF: Don't die, Leo. It's a waste of time.

MISCHA: *(To CLAIRE.)* Betrayed…

MONTCRIEFF: Give birth to something…

MISCHA: …birth…

MONTCRIEFF: …money, gardens, cities…

MISCHA: …trust…

MONTCRIEFF: …wine, food, clothes…

MISCHA: … love…

MONTCRIEFF: …theories, chaos – anything…

MISCHA: …friends…

MONTCRIEFF: …Anything to give meaning to this helpless, weird and wonderful life!

MISCHA: …everything!

MONTCRIEFF: You hear me, Leo?

MISCHA: *(To MINERVA.)* Betrayed us and everything!

MINERVA: Speak for yourself!

MONTCRIEFF: Birth!

MINERVA: Your friend is in pain, for God's sake.

MISCHA: Your friend has destroyed, for God's sake.

MONTCRIEFF: Give birth!

> *Lights out on all three areas of VINCENT, LEO, and MONTCRIEFF.*

SCENE TWELVE

> *The WOMEN are held as though paralysed by an explosion in their midst.*
>
> *CLAIRE especially is on the verge of 'flipping'.*
>
> *The dust of revelation settles.*
>
> *They are not the friends they were when the play began. Each is embarrassed.*
>
> *MISCHA and MINERVA sit somewhere where they can pretend they are at ease.*

MISCHA: Perhaps a brandy?

MINERVA: Perhaps I should take up smoking again.

CLAIRE: Perhaps I should go home.

> *The atmosphere is tense. No one moves.*

MINERVA: *(To CLAIRE.) Is* Vincent destroyed?

CLAIRE: I don't know…I don't think so…perhaps…

MISCHA: He's been caught lying before three and a half million people for God's sake.

CLAIRE: *(With no conviction.)* He has charm…he can…

MISCHA: Charm? Charm? With every major politician watching?

CLAIRE: He'll plead human frailty…

MISCHA: They will devour him.

CLAIRE: ...explain he was protecting the sensibilities of his mistress...

MISCHA: And what will his mistress explain?

MINERVA: That the man's a shit, a coward, an opportunist who placed career before other people's feelings – I hope.

Silence.

MISCHA: Claire?

MINERVA: Is she on trial here?

MISCHA: If we're to continue a friendship we've got to talk.

MINERVA: To say what?

MISCHA: To say why!

MINERVA: I don't think Claire needs to justify herself.

MISCHA: Justification is not the issue.

MINERVA: What is?

MISCHA: Values.

MINERVA: What values? Vincent employed Claire as his researcher, seduced her, used her, then dumped her as a threat to his political career.

MISCHA: Is that how Claire sees it?

MINERVA: How else can she see it?

MISCHA: Let Claire answer.

MINERVA: Maybe it's Claire's affair.

MISCHA: No. It's mine too. I introduced her to Vincent. She came with my recommendation and my blessing. I have a right to know.

MINERVA: What's there to know? She was a woman in love?

MISCHA: Which justifies all behaviour?

MINERVA: *Explains* all behaviour.

MISCHA: Explains what? Treachery?

MINERVA: You're talking reason, Mischa. Love is a pain, rejection is a pain. People in pain are not reasonable.

MISCHA: Perhaps we should parade the seductive myth of women's emotions. Those tender creatures who feel more deeply than men and can't be expected to use their head.

MINERVA: That most definitely is *not* what I'm saying. I'm talking about pain right across the board. For both women and men. Pain is pain is pain is pain is pain.

MISCHA: Pain or no pain I have a hard time reconciling love with betrayal.

MINERVA: And when love is withdrawn?

MISCHA: We don't love only because we're loved.

MINERVA: We love better, though.

MISCHA: But not less. I question the nature of a love that wants to destroy because love is withdrawn.

MINERVA: Then you've never known those women who rage, smash windows, break furniture, set fire to homes, make scenes in public, howl outside doors at night, put shit through letter boxes, poison the natural affection of children, parade them in the early hours before their father's mistress, threaten murder, suicide, and sometimes more than threaten.

MISCHA: Did *you* do any of those things when Montcrieff left *you*?

MINERVA: I wanted to.

MISCHA: But *did* you? *Did* you?

> *Silence.*

Then why do you condone what Claire has done? Is it because she's done it for you, perhaps?

MINERVA: That's cheap. No, it's because he spat her out when she no longer suited his purpose. Crime and punishment. Someone wrote a book about it.

MISCHA: It is no crime to choose a new direction in life. That's everyone's right. If my new love wakes up one morning and decides to move out I will hurt to the core of my being but I *would* not, *could* not find it in me to punish him.

MINERVA: Say you don't know, dearly beloved, say cautiously, carefully, fearful of your unpredictable heart that you-just-do-not-know.

MISCHA: I know!

MINERVA: You can't know.

MISCHA: I can and do. What – to dare presume that he *had* to continue loving me? The arrogance of it! 'Me! Me! You must love only me!' I would be ashamed.

MINERVA: We are not talking of a man who loved but of a man who used. Callously used.

MISCHA: Well, let's look closely at that. 'Used'? Is that the word you'd employ, Claire? 'Used'?

MINERVA: All rejection makes you feel used.

MISCHA: Whose salary almost doubled? Who met some of the most illustrious minds of Europe? Who travelled to places undreamt of? Who's gained a wealth of experience, connections, influence?

MINERVA: The greater the pain of rejection.

MISCHA: Oh no! You can't have it both ways. Either her pain comes from being exploited or it comes from withdrawal of the good life.

MINERVA: Either way one feels used.

MISCHA: Used! An emotive word which blurs the truth.

MINERVA: Oh, and what is the truth, wise Mischa?

MISCHA: Neither dramatic nor consoling. Passion is ephemeral, an exotic plant with a short life-span. It chokes on its own succulence.

MINERVA: And love? Love? We all know about short-lived passion but what about love?

MISCHA: *(To CLAIRE.)* Love? Let's look closely at that, too. How did he break it to you, Claire? Coldly on the phone?

CLAIRE: No.

MISCHA: The inevitable, cruel letter of regret?

CLAIRE shakes her head.

MINERVA: How, then?

CLAIRE: Over dinner.

MISCHA: Face to face?

CLAIRE: Face to face.

MISCHA: Courageously face to face?

CLAIRE: Courageously face to face.

MINERVA: What does it matter how he told her? He told her! 'Over! Done! You've had your fun, it's the wife and children now.'

MISCHA: And had Montcrieff returned and said 'it's the wife and children now' you'd have opened your arms, blessed him, said he'd come to his senses and was an honourable man after all. Yes? No?

MINERVA: You are missing the point.

MISCHA: Oh, and what is the point, wise Minerva?

MINERVA: Love is a vow, in or out of marriage it's a commitment. A woman who loves surrenders herself totally, completely, utterly. It can't be treated lightly.

MISCHA: Who treated it lightly?

MINERVA: Vincent stopped loving a woman who passionately loved him.

MISCHA: Oh, so it *was* love? She *wasn't* used?

MINERVA: You're deliberately not understanding me. Used is what's left when loving stops.

CLAIRE: Loving didn't stop.

Both her friends turn to her.

MISCHA: Loving didn't stop?

CLAIRE: Loving didn't stop. He didn't stop loving me. He loves me still, I know. It's just that – it was that – I think that –

She is like one dazed.

– there was – such intensity. Of feeling. Of conversation. Of laughter. Of shared judgements and shared wicked joys. We mocked the same humbug, admired the same talents, marvelled at the same courage in colleagues. We generated each other's energy, built unspoken rhythms, gave each other space. I was dependable, discrete, undemanding. And then – one day – withdrawn! As if nothing had ever happened.

She fights to hold back hysteria.

How could that be? We had come together as if by design. No doubts, no hesitations. Locked! Engaged! Instantly. Precision-made. An efficient machine to the world, an unexpected gift to ourselves. It was terrifying. Can't be true, we thought. Can't last. We'll be found out, caught. One of us will have an accident. A child will die. We'd have to pay for such happiness, surely. Surely we'd have to pay. No one deserves what the Gods were bestowing upon us, we thought.

So what happened? I couldn't understand. The man who rejected me couldn't be the man I loved or who loved me, I reasoned. He was somebody else.

There is madness in this.

What I did, I did to somebody else. I talked to the television researchers about somebody else.

That was right, wasn't it? That makes sense? Do you imagine I'd hurt the man I love?

She is going over the edge.

Do you really imagine I'd hurt the man I love? Hurt the man I love? *Hurt?* The man I love? The man I *love?* Love? Love? Hurt the man I love…?

She is gone.

HER FRIENDS move either side to comfort her.

FADE.

The End.

WILD SPRING

a play in two acts

Characters

GERTRUDE MATTHEWS
a well-known actress who ages 44 to 59.

SAMSON MARTIN
black, aged 19, a theatre car park attendant.

KENNEDY PHILLIPS
black, aged around 30,
theatre company manager.

Note

For companies outside the UK where there is no
black community the play will be as effective, with
minor modifications, played to represent any group
of outsiders – for example: Arabs in France; Turks in
Germany; Gypsies everywhere!

Time and Place

The play, except for one scene, is set in London
over a period of fifteen years.

ACT ONE is set in 1976

ACT TWO is set in 1991

Settings

Act One

Act Two

'...the childishly egotistical character of her acting, which is not the art of making you think more highly or feel more deeply, but the art of making you admire her, pity her, champion her, weep with her, laugh at her jokes, follow her fortunes breathlessly, and applaud her wildly when the curtain falls. It is the art of finding out all your weaknesses and practising on them – cajoling you, harrowing you, exciting you – on the whole fooling you...

George Bernard Shaw on Sarah Bernhardt
from *Dramatic Opinions and Essays – Volume 1*

Act One

SCENE ONE

Spring 1976.

Actress, GERTRUDE MATTHEWS, (we will call her GERTIE) with her back to us, is performing Lear's Fool to an unseen audience. (Act 3 Sc. 2)

MUSIC is building through it.

GERTIE: *This is a brave night to cool a courtezan.*
    I'll speak a prophecy ere I go:
    When priests are more in word than matter;
    When brewers mar their malt with water;
    When nobles are their tailors' tutors;
    No heretics burn'd, but wenches' suitors;
    When every case in law is right;
    No squire in debt, nor no poor knight;
    When slanders do not live in tongues;
    Nor cut purses come not to throngs;
    When usurers tell their gold i'the field;
    And bawds and whores do churches build;
    Then shall the realm of Albion
    Come to great confusion:
    Then comes the time, who lives to see't,
    That going shall be us'd with feet
    This prophecy Merlin shall make: for I live before his time.

        MUSIC at its height.
        Lights down.

SCENE TWO

GERTIE's dressing-rooms. Sound of applause. The play has ended.

GERTIE, petite, pugnaciously pretty, enters from the room where she has been disrobing, only the Fool's cap on her head remains from her costume. The rest is underwear.

She is buoyant, bubbling. Pours herself a whisky.

She talks to her unseen dresser, Lottie, in the other room through which comes a general back-stage buzz.

GERTIE: My God, didn't they love all that tonight. A woman playing the Fool! They'll go home and tell their family and friends 'do you know, the Fool was played by Gertie Mathews, a woman! Fantastic!'

In front of the mirror.

Sharp! Sharp, sharp, sharp!

To 'Lottie'.

That's it, Lottie. I won't be needing anything else. Don't hang about. See you tomorrow.

Closes door. Turns down tannoy. Starts to take off make-up. Singing.

When that I was and a little tiny boy
With hey, ho the wind and the rain...

No! Stop that, Gertie! You can't carry the play around with you everywhere. Leave it alone, on stage, wash it out of your hair.

(Singing.)

I'm gonna wash ole Shakespeare out of my hair
I'm gonna wash ole Shakespeare out of my hair
I'm gonna wash ole Shakespeare out of my hair
Gonna send him on his way.

(Closing her eyes.) If I close my eyes I can see everything that's wonderful about being alive.

You're in good spirits tonight, Gertie. What's happened? *(Pause.)* I'll give you three guesses. *(Pause.)* You've been asked to take over the company. God forbid! Confront actor's egos all day every day? *(Pause.)* You've discovered your mother is not really your mother, you were adopted. Ha! Wouldn't *that* change my life. *(Pause.)* You're going to be laid tonight. Wrong again! That would put me in very high spirits indeed, but all the men are dead as far as I can make out. Or emigrated. *(Pause.)* What, then? *(Pause.)* I'll tell you what then, you were stunning tonight, that's fucking what then. You were one hundred per cent in tune with your Fool and you knew it and they knew it and you knew they knew it, and they knew you knew and they loved you and you loved them and everybody loved everybody and it was electric and fantastic. Fan-fucking-tastic. *(Pause.)* Gawd! That's terrible! To be so dependent upon praise. To be so dependent upon the praise of an audience for your happiness – that's a shameful confession. Just a little love and admiration from anybody and you're anybody's!

> *Make-up is off. Contemplates herself in the mirror.*

'You walk like a crab' said my ballet teacher when my mother took me to classes, aged eight. 'I hope you don't dance like one.' *Do* I walk like a crab?

> *She stands and walks, slightly sideways.*

I suppose I do. But not on stage. On stage, Gertie Matthews, you're something else. Crab off stage but on stage – goddess!

> *Knock on her door.*

Enter!

SAMSON MARTIN, black, the theatre's car-park attendant, pokes his head round door catching her in a 'goddess' stance.

Her deified posture and scant dress startles him.

SAM: Sorry, Miss Matthews. I'll come back.

GERTIE: It's OK, Sam. I may be half undressed but by the same token I'm half dressed.

She reaches for an old, exotic dressing-gown.

SAM: I thought you'd be finished, Miss, so I brought your car–keys.

GERTIE: You knew very well I wouldn't be finished, the applause is still ringing in our ears. Come in, sit down, pour yourself a whisky and prepare to listen to a lecture I'm going to give you.

SAM: I keep telling you, Miss Matthews, I don't like whisky.

GERTIE: What *do* you like?

SAM: I keep telling you, Miss Matthews, I like Coke.

GERTIE: Take a Coke then, and listen. You didn't come to give me car keys. You normally give me my car keys as soon as you've parked the car – for which I'm very grateful because the car-park is meant for the audience not the players so I hope you do it very surreptitiously –

SAM: What's 'surreptitiously', Miss Mathews?

GERTIE: Stop that! How many times must I tell you don't play ignorant you're not good at it so I hope you do it very surreptitiously because I don't want you getting into trouble on my account. No! You came to share my company. You've got good taste – you like me. I've got good taste – I like you. We like each other. *You're* too young and *I'm* too old for this to be passion but let's be grateful for small blessings and try to be honest with one another.

SAM: I *was* being honest.

GERTIE: *(Ignoring him.)* My mum made *me* a liar because she didn't let me go out with the friends I liked, so I learned to lie like a chameleon. But you and me –

SAM: I *was* being honest..

GERTIE: You weren't.

SAM: I was.

GERTIE: You weren't

SAM: Was.

GERTIE: Weren't

SAM: Was.

GERTIE: Weren't.

SAM: Was.

GERTIE: Wasn't.

SAM: 'Wasn't?'

GERTIE: Yes. Wasn't. What's wrong with 'wasn't'?

SAM: Sounds funny.

GERTIE: Wasn't – was not.

SAM: You 'was not' being honest?

GERTIE: Didn't they teach you at school about the fun of playing with words?

SAM: Might've done. I wasn't listening.

GERTIE: You listened well enough to know 'wasn't' was incorrect.

SAM: I didn't *know* it, it just *sounded* wrong.

She goes into the other room to change.

GERTIE: And the other reason for being honest is that the English mostly aren't, and if you want to get on in this cold and hostile society you've got to build a reputation for honesty.

SAM: Are you always honest, Miss Matthews?

GERTIE: No! Do you think I'm crazy? I'm a woman, an actress, and white. As a woman if I were honest I'd never be able to hold a man; as an actress I get paid not to be honest; and being white *I* can get away with murder – but as you're black –

Peeps round door.

– you *are* black aren't you?

SAM: No, miss, I just haven't washed.

GERTIE: Oh, sharp! Sharp, sharp, sharp!

Returns to continue changing.

– but as you're black you've got to be twice as virtuous.

Long pause before she reappears.

Christ! I do talk nonsense, don't I? It's all more complex than that.

SAM: What does 'complex' mean?

GERTIE: Will you please *stop* that? You know perfectly well what 'complex' means. Pretending you're a car-park attendant! Do you enjoy the image of yourself as a 'car-park attendant'? People are always creating an image of themselves which they fall in love with and then can't get rid of. I'm encased in this image my mum inspired, bless her.

SAM: What image is that, Miss Matthews?

GERTIE: 'Don't you go thinking *you've* got talent, Gertie, it's just God's gift.' Not a bad image to fall in love with, modesty.

SAM: If it's true.

GERTIE: Sharp, sharp, sharp! But in your case it's not. You've confused modesty for self-denigration – don't you dare ask me what 'self-denigration' is – and if you're not careful,

Sam-my-son, Samson, you'll persuade yourself you can't be anything else but a car-park attendant. Frozen! For the rest of your life! Car-park attendant! Unable to discard it even though God might have wanted you to be an astronaut. I, on the other hand, get paid for falling love with countless images of myself which I can later discard. Where was I?

SAM: 'It's all more complex than that'.

GERTIE: Thank you. It's all more complex than that.

> *Pause.*

What's more complex than what?

SAM: Needing to be twice as virtuous because you're black.

GERTIE: Oh yes. Did I say that?

SAM: 'Fraid so.

GERTIE: Well, it's *some*times true. The point is: there are no rules in life. One or two laws, like 'thou shalt not kill'; or 'fall off Big Ben and you'll hurt yourself'. But no rules. You make life up as you go along. You lie to those who can't take the truth or don't deserve the truth, but when you find special friends, like me, you're honest. Understood?

SAM: And can I lie to protect others?

GERTIE: Only if those others deserve protecting.

SAM: What if they're friends who've done wrong?

GERTIE: That's a moral dilemma you'll have to face yourself. I'm no philosopher.

SAM: What's 'a moral dilemma'?

GERTIE: If you keep asking stupid questions I'll hit you.

SAM: I'm only a car-park attendant, you know.

GERTIE: Stop weeping for yourself. Now, my friend, I must rush. My son's waiting to be tucked up and kissed to sleep and then I've got a dinner date with colleagues who need me to organise a committee for good works and I'm a good organiser who loves being needed so off I go and why don't you come and have Sunday lunch with me one day so's you can get to meet Tom.

SAM seems uncertain.

He's only a mongol, not a vampire.

SAM: Cor! You don't half make jokes about strange things.

GERTIE: It's called 'black humour' – a way of surviving.

SAM: How old is he?

GERTIE: Seven. Now *he's* my passion. You'll love him. Everyone does. Will you? Sunday lunch? See how the other half lives?

SAM: You're always making me do things I shouldn't be doing.

GERTIE: 'Shouldn't'?

SAM: You get me to eat food I ain't never eaten before, you get me to see plays which make my friends laugh at me, you buy me ties I don't have the shirts to go with. You even make me read books! When I leave you and go home I don't know who I am.

GERTIE: Join the club!

SAM: I'm serious.

GERTIE: OK. You're a car-park attendant. I'll try to remember that. You were born to be a theatre car-park attendant. Come for Sunday lunch and I'll make you hamburgers and chips.

SAM: I mean, it's not right to make someone what they're not.

GERTIE: It's worse to *imagine* you're someone you're not. I've got to go.

SAM: I mean, it's all right for people like you, Miss Matthews, you're famous, you're needed, you know where you're going.

GERTIE: Yes, and I've got to go there, Sam. We'll talk later.

SAM: I mean you don't know what it's like to –

GERTIE: I know very well what 'it's like to' but I've got to go. Sunday lunch. Hamburgers and chips. No patés. Promise.

> *She leaves.*

> *SAM looks around. He loves the atmosphere of dressing rooms.*

SAM: She trusts you, Sam. You could pinch her watch which she's forgotten. *(Pockets her watch.)* You could steal this antique coffee cup which'd fetch a bob or two. *(Pockets cup.)* I bet this old print is worth something. *(Slips it into his overalls.)*

(Imitating her.) 'My mum made *me* a liar because she didn't let me go out with the friends I liked, so I lie like a chameleon. But you and me – 'She's always talking about her mum. 'My mum was a manipulator...' 'What's a manipulator, Miss Matthews?' 'My dad was hungry for affection but my mum was emotionally parsimonious...' 'What's 'parsimonious', Miss Matthews?' 'Gertie hasn't got looks, said my mum, but she's got character...'

She has, too. Aren't you lucky I like you, Miss Matthews. *(Returns print.)* Aren't you lucky I'm your friend, Miss Matthews. *(Returns cup.)* Aren't you lucky you can trust me, Miss Matthews. *(Returns watch.)* I've got a mum, too, and she tell me 'You steal, boy, and you end up messing your only life. And don't think 'cos I'm your mum I'll come running to bail you out, 'cos I won't.' So, Miss Matthews, we both got mums.

> *He says it in such a way that we're not certain.*

(Closing his eyes.) If I close my eyes I can hear my head thinking.

> *He places the Fool's hat on his head. Preens himself. He's no actor but he's heard the lines many times.*

This is a brave night to cool a courtezan –
I'll speak a prophesy ere I go...'
'You steal, boy, and you end up messing your only life.'
Good ole mum.

> *He makes a joyful leap in the air, kicking his feet*
> *together.*

You enjoy being trusted don't you, Sam boy?

> *Another leap.*

> *Sound of applause.*

> *Taking off hat, he bows.*

> *The applause belongs to –*

SCENE THREE

An award ceremony.

GERTIE stands before a microphone clutching a
statue. She's crippled with embarrassment to have
won.

GERTIE: Well. What do I say? I know – that's what everyone
asks: 'what do I say?' and then everyone thanks everyone.
And I do. Everyone. Thank them… Oh dear – you can tell
I didn't expect to win, I'm not prepared. Bit strange really.
This. Such a coveted award. Just for playing the Fool. I
should have lots of them if that's all it takes.

> *Waits for laughter.*

I don't know…I'm…I'm…honoured. You all know that.
It's more than honour though, isn't it? If we're truthful
it's also vindication. Your work and your faith have been
vindicated. You've proved them wrong. Them! Those
loving doubters. My mum, bless her, she meant well, but
my mum used to say 'Gertie hasn't got looks but she's
got character'. 'Character'. So, I win awards playing
the Fool. Ha! Yes. Well. Vindicated. And justified. You
hold something like this in your hand and you feel your

existence is justified. As though you've earned the air you're breathing. I'd better stop now – I'll get even sillier or weep. Thank you.

> *She offers an unexpected and sweet curtsey.*
>
> *Applause.*
>
> *Over it comes the voice and laughter of a mongol child. It's a moving and joyful sound.*
>
> *Mixed in with it is GERTIE's voice.*

SCENE FOUR

> *GERTIE's dining room.*
>
> *Mixed styles, elegant, orderly. Full of memorabilia.*
>
> *SAM is at table. Lunch is finished.*

GERTIE'S VOICE: Enough now, Tom. You've played with Sam and it's time for a sleep. Yes yes yes of course I love you. Yes, I know, and you love me. Sing to you? But I can't leave Sam all alone out there. *(Calling.)* Sam, you all right for a minute?

SAM: Fine, Miss Matthews.

GERTIE'S VOICE: Have some more ice-cream-cake if you want. *(To TOM.)* OK now, Tom. Just once. Promise if I sing it that you won't ask me to sing it again. Just once. Promise?

> *GERTIE sings Freste's song from Twelfth Night, Act V, scene 1.*

'*When that I was and a little tiny boy,*
With hey, ho the wind and the rain,
A foolish thing was but a toy,
For the rain it raineth every day.
With hey, ho the wind and the rain,
For the rain it raineth every day.

> *While she sings the remaining verses off stage SAM executes some tai chi movements. Slow, surprising and beautiful.*
>
> *GERTIE has obviously succeeded in singing her son to sleep because she's backing out of his room with the last lines.*
>
> *A touching scene – singing mother with her back to us, SAM, oblivious, doing his Chinese exercises.*
>
> *She turns and watches him a while until he realises the singing has stopped. He turns and sees her watching. He's embarrassed.*

GERTIE: I thought you were only the car-park attendant.

SAM: I'm the car-park attendant what can do tai chi, en I?

GERTIE: Can you teach me some movements?

SAM: Easy.

GERTIE: Go on, then.

SAM: Now?

GERTIE: Never put off till tomorrow what can be done today, my mum used to say. Pretty stupid saying I thought, but not always.

SAM: Try this.

> *He demonstrates an elementary movement. She follows.*
>
> *Another. She follows.*
>
> *A third. She follows.*

GERTIE: I think I could become attached to this.

> *She repeats them on her own a number of times, talking meanwhile.*

I didn't know anything was wrong with him for ages. He was just weeks old when I adopted him and the silly

buggers in the adoption centre hadn't seen it. We took one
look at each other, Tom and me, and fell in love. Couple
of months later I took him for a routine check-up to our
doctor who said nothing to me – because of course I was
only the mother, a woman – but he rang my husband.
'You've adopted a mongol child'. Chilling news chillingly
delivered. Chilled my husband. Chilled him for days.
Then one morning at ten o'clock, two hours before a
dress rehearsal of 'Three Sisters' he blurted it out. 'We've
adopted a mongol child.' Buggered up rehearsals I can
tell you. Halfway through I broke down and the director
yelled at me 'I know you've had heartbreaking news but
thank your lucky stars you've got your work so GET ON
WITH IT!'

SAM: Why did your old man tell you on the day of a dress
rehearsal?

GERTIE: Well you may ask. *I* never understood. But then there
were a lot of things I didn't understand about my husband.
Of course our doctor was furious. He wanted to write
letters all over the place but it was too late – we loved Tom
too much by then.

She stops her tai chi movements.

Cor! Reveals muscles you didn't know you had. *(Pause.)*
So, I never go anywhere without seeing him every night to
sleep. Sleeps a lot does Tom. Very energetic awake, very
still asleep. *(Beat.)* Wadja think? Didn't you love him?

SAM: Yeah. But *I* don't have to be with him all the time.

GERTIE: I *can't* be with him all the time. Costs a bomb for
a nanny. *(Pause.)* What do you see when you close your
eyes?

SAM does so. Thinks about it.

SAM: Dying images of what I saw just before I closed them!

GERTIE: Will you never give a straight answer?

SAM: What you taking such a friendly interest in me for?

GERTIE: Friends don't ask questions like that. Friends know they're friends.

SAM: 'Friends', Miss Matthews?

GERTIE: I think it's about time you called me 'Gertie'.

SAM: I like calling you Miss Matthews.

GERTIE: Suit yourself.

SAM: Friends? Me nineteen you forty-four?

GERTIE: How did you know my age?

SAM: I didn't. You just told me.

GERTIE: Oh sharp. Sharp, sharp, sharp!

SAM: You ain't doing good deeds are you, Miss Matthews? Me black, you white?

GERTIE: Yes. Of course I'm doing good deeds. What's wrong with good deeds?

SAM: People should do what makes them happy not what makes them look good.

GERTIE: Good deeds *make* me happy and I *like* looking good! Jesus, what's got into you, Sam?

SAM: My mum always told me 'Beware of Good-Deed-Doers'.

GERTIE: Well, mums are a mixed blessing. We all know that.

SAM: You do a lot of good deeds?

GERTIE: Can't do enough of them. You ask me, I'll do it. Makes up for all the bad deeds I do.

SAM: Bad deeds? You?

GERTIE: You really probe don't you?

SAM: Not bad for a car-park attendant you mean?

GERTIE: A car-park attendant!

SAM: Well, some's got it and some ain't.

GERTIE: Haven't.

SAM: Haven't.

GERTIE: And you – haven't.

SAM: To be what? See me acting? See me painting? See me being an architect, a doctor, a lawyer, a politician, a deep-sea diver?

GERTIE: The alternative is being a car-park attendant?

SAM: If I can't be any of those things…

GERTIE: A car-park attendant! Nice image to fall in love with.

SAM: Aren't you in love with *your* image? Good-Deed-Doer?

GERTIE: Probe *and* hurt. Yes. I enjoy the image of myself being useful. Nothing useful about being an actor. Once you know you can do it you just go on doing it. The audience applauds, goes home, and you're left wondering what you did. Played a role. Someone else's words. Someone else's image.

SAM: Which you fell in love with!

GERTIE: Oh sharp. Sharp, sharp, sharp!

SAM: For a car-park attendant.

GERTIE: That really is a chip and a half on your shoulder.

SAM: Got lots more where that came from.

GERTIE: How fortunate you are. Wish I had a few chips to lean on. I've got nothing to complain about and no one to blame.

SAM: Except your mum.

GERTIE: Well mums are always a good stand-by for off-loading blame. Problem with my mum was she taught me to blame myself. For everything. 'Don't annoy people, don't contradict them, don't ask favours, don't lose your temper,

don't complain, don't bang doors…' She made me feel I
had to apologise for the air I breathed.

She was tiny. Very tiny. And strong. Gave my poor dad a
rough ole time – worked for a boot and shoe factory as a
commercial traveller. Hated it. I only ever saw him when
he came home at weekends so mum and I went twice
a week to the pictures and I spent the rest of my time
imagining I was Doris Day or Marlene Dietrich. They were
second cousins, you know. Mum and dad, that is, not Doris
and Marlene. Dad thought she was a saint. Not Marlene,
mum. She only married him to please *her* mum. Mum's
mum, that is, not Marlene's. *(Beat.)* You do know who
Marlene Dietrich and Doris Day are, don't you.

> *SAM nods his head but says 'No'.*

How do you do that?

> *She shakes her head but can only say 'no', nod it
> and only say 'yes'.*

I can't do it.

> *SAM gives another demonstration shaking and
> nodding his head and saying the contrary word.*

Stop it! Makes me dizzy.

SAM: Go on telling me about your mum.

GERTIE: 'The only person in the world worth loving is
your mother.' Subtle! Never understood the possibility
you might meet someone else. And as for sex. 'It's all
disgusting, and women never enjoy it!'

SAM: Learned about it from books did you?

GERTIE: Books? *Books?* There *were* no books in the house.
You weren't supposed to *read*. I joined Boot's library and
read under the bedclothes with a torch. No books, no
conversation, no social conscience, no sex. Just guilts.
There was so much I shouldn't do that I did and lied

about, it was such a don't-do-this-or-that upbringing that I was riddled with guilts. And so if anything goes wrong I know it's me who's made it go wrong. You may have noticed – I walk like a crab, as though there's always something to avoid. You're lucky. You're black. You can blame everybody for everything. I've got no one except myself to blame, at which I am an expert, believe me. So you stay a car-park attendant, Sam, you can blame a car-park attendant's life on a whole number of things. Cosy. Try to be something more you might fail then you'll have to blame yourself. Not so cosy.

SAM: You *are* a talker aren't you, Miss Matthews?

GERTIE: Thank you.

SAM: I like listening to you.

GERTIE: Thank you.

SAM: Even though you don't always make sense.

GERTIE: Thank you.

SAM: Why don't I always make sense, Sam?

GERTIE: Why don't I always make sense, Sam?

SAM: I'm glad you asked me that, Miss Matthews. Your mum made you feel everything was your fault, right?

GERTIE: Right.

SAM: She was wrong to make you feel everything was your fault, right?

GERTIE: Right.

SAM: But you think I should try to be more than a car-park attendant so that if I fail it can only be my fault, right?

GERTIE: Right.

SAM: So your mum was wrong to make you blame yourself, but you're right to want me in a situatioin where only I can take the blame, right?

GERTIE: Right.

SAM: How can two contradictory situations both be right?

GERTIE: Because that's life.

SAM: You don't let me get away with nothing.

GERTIE: Anything.

SAM: Nothing.

GERTIE: If I *don't* let you get away with nothing it means I *do* let you get away with something. So – anything.

SAM: See what I mean?

GERTIE: Oh, sharp. Sharp, sharp, sharp.

SAM: *(Shaking his head.)* Oh, yes, yes, yes.

GERTIE: Stop that! Stop it!

SCENE FIVE

A beach.

High winds. Raging sea. Exhilarating.

Nearby – a rock.

GERTIE's voice calling above the sound.

GERTIE'S VOICE: Sam! Sam! Don't get too near. An unexpected wave could grab and drag you down to old Davy's locker.

> *She appears on the rock, warmly dressed for gales.*

'*Blow, winds, and crack your cheeks! rage! blow!*
You cataracts and hurricanoes, spout
Till you have drench'd our steeples, drown'd the cocks!'*

> *Pause to call again.*

Sam! Sam!

'You sulph'rous and thought-executing fires.
Vaunt couriers of oak-cleaving thunderbolts,
Singe my white head! And thou, all shaking thunder,
Strike flat the thick rotundity o' the world!
Crack Nature's moulds, all germens spill at once,
That make ingrateful man!'

> *SAM, similarly dressed and with a haversack, has appeared during this and stood, as audience, looking up.*
>
> *They must shout at each other to be heard.*

I should have played Lear, not his fool. Wadya think?

SAM: As a king or a queen?

GERTIE: A queen. Queen Leah and her three sons. Question is – would a queen have been as stupid as a king and not recognised the sweet honesty of her youngest son?

SAM: Women's intuition, right!

GERTIE: If *my* youngest son told me, 'I love you according to my bond, no more no less' I'd know exactly what he meant.

SAM: Which is why the old bard made Lear a man, didn't he? Have a woman – there'd be no play.

GERTIE: *(Referring to the high winds.)* Exhilarating, isn't it.

SAM: Yeah. Wild.

GERTIE: Help me down.

> *He does so.*
>
> *From the haversack he withdraws a groundsheet, lays it in a sheltered part of the rock.*
>
> *GERTIE dips into the haversack for a hip flask and a Coke. They sit to drink.*
>
> *The sound of the elements fades.*

GERTIE: *(Referring to brandy.)* I knew this would come in handy.

She unscrews and pours.

SAM: When did you know you was going to be an actress?

GERTIE: When I was three years old I announced 'I, Gertrude Matthews, am going to be a fairy.' Cheers. *(Drinks.)*

SAM: Cheers. Simple as that? *(Drinks.)*

GERTIE: Nothing's as simple as that. I caught double pneumonia at two and lost the use of my legs. Had to be taught to walk again. Doctor advised dancing lessons. Pah poum! Start of brilliant career.

SAM: 'I, Gertrude Matthews, am going to be a fairy'. Sounds easy. 'I, Samson Martin, am going to be a – '

GERTIE: A what?

SAM: Well, not a fairy, that's for sure.

GERTIE: A car-park attendant. We know.

SAM: Yeah. I forgot. 'I, Samson Martin, am going to be a car-park attendant.'

GERTIE: In sickness and in health, for better or for worse ...

SAM: Till death do us part.

GERTIE: Amen.

SAM: So, you decided to be a fairy. What then?

Long pause.

GERTIE: When I close my eyes *(She does.)* I can see Palmers Green. The tiny, dreary, two-up two-down behind the curtains of which, wrote the poet, are people living out their lives of quiet desperation. I don't think my mum knew she was doing that but when I close my eyes I can smell the acrid smell of the kitchen range which she'd painted silver. She *was.* Quietly desperate. Nothing pleased her. She found joy in no one and no thing.

There *was* a time when she got excited. The early days. When I close my eyes I can see dad frantically making props and mum sewing on sequins for my first dress in my first public appearance – Miss Milligan's Dancing Display. But there was this girl called Renee Harmer, 'the Harmer Girl', and when I close my eyes I can hear mum saying 'if only you smiled like the Harmer girl. Renee Harmer is so pretty. You watch the Harmer girl, *she'll* go places.' Practised like the furies but it wasn't enough for my mum.

When I close my eyes I can see photographers flashing. I can see mum taking my make-up off with margarine. I can hear the compliments of anyone who was anyone in North London. And all ending, every Saturday, year in year out, eating raisin-sandwiches and drinking cocoa.

When I close my eyes I can see my dad painting. Landscapes. That's all he wanted to be – a landscape painter. He was a dreamer with never enough talent to make his dreams come true but just enough sense never to wake up.

When I close my eyes I can see every blister like a medal, feel every headache like tokens of triumph.

    Long pause.

What do you see when you close *your* eyes?

SAM: When I close my eyes *(Closes them.)* – hills. Purple hills. Behind me. In front – a beach. All sand. No stones. No stones and no people. I'm lying flat on my back. Bermuda shorts, pattern from playing cards – red diamonds, black spades, red hearts, black clubs. My eyes are closed. Suddenly – I feel a snake. Crawling over me. Up my leg, my sides, under my armpit. It stays there. Curled-up and snug. I'm terrified. Can't move. Can't open my eyes. Hours pass. Hours and hours and hours. It's night. I can hear the tide getting closer. And closer. And closer. Water's touching my feet. Covering my legs. I've got to move. I've *got* to. I move. The snake bites. I die.

Long pause.

GERTIE: Try again.

SAM: When I close my eyes – screaming. Dad beats mum. Mum beats sister. Sister beats me. I beat brothers. Blood. When I close my eyes – blood and screaming. No one listens. No one to no one. Screaming. Blood.

GERTIE: Too purple. Too pretentious. Try again.

SAM: When I close my eyes –

With eyes closed he struggles.

when I close my eyes –

Struggles more.

when I close my eyes –

Struggle turns to distress as though he were an epileptic, which he's not.

GERTIE feels she must hold him or he'll explode.

He nestles in her arms, calmed.

When I close my eyes I'm all feeling. Can't see *anything* really. Can't think anything either.

GERTIE: Maybe you *hear* instead? Family voices?

He thinks about this.

SAM: 'Where you going, mum?'
'Out! Away from you bloody lot.'
'Don't go, mum. I'll keep them quiet.'
'What, this brood? Quiet? Not till hell freezes over'.
'Where you going, dad?'
'Out'
'Out where?'

'Just out! Anywhere but here.'
'Don't go, dad. We'll paint the living room.'
'You all give me grief, you know that? Grief!'

GERTIE: Feudin' family, huh?

SAM: Nah! Everybody loved everybody, only nobody loved themselves.

GERTIE: Unlike the English who hate each other and love only themselves. And even then not much.

SAM: Not true. Some of my best friends are English.

GERTIE: Like me?

SAM: Yeah. Like you.

> *He kisses her lightly on the lips.*
>
> *It's a moment.*

I've never had a white woman.

GERTIE: You're not having one now.

SAM: You mean that's it? One kiss?

GERTIE: You can have another if you like, even a third if you promise not to catch fire, but nothing more.

SAM: Wrong colour?

GERTIE: Wrong age.

SAM: I don't think you're too old.

GERTIE: Thank you. But I think you're too young. Find someone your own age.

SAM: I don't like young girls.

GERTIE: It's time to go, Sam.

SAM: All they think about is sex.

GERTIE: Disgusting.

SAM: I like women who've lived.

GERTIE: Weather-beaten, you mean. On your feet.

SAM: This the brush-off, then?

GERTIE: Don't be dramatic.

SAM: Did I tell you my mum died?

GERTIE: *(Sympathetically.)* Oh, Sam.

SAM: My dad won the premium bonds. Hundred thousand pounds. Ran off with the lot. Broke my mum's heart. Gave her cancer.

GERTIE: You're lying.

SAM: We never heard from him again.

GERTIE: You mustn't lie about such things, they come true.

SAM: Sent me off the rails, I can tell you.

GERTIE: I'm not listening to your lies. They upset me.

SAM: Started robbing Paki newsagents and pushing white girls around.

GERTIE: I think there's a storm coming up.

SAM: They nabbed me in the end. Three years detention.

           No response.

Where I found God.

           No response.

Joined the Salvation Army when I came out.

GERTIE: Are you going to stop?

SAM: Are you going to kiss me?

GERTIE: This spring's getting too wild for me. My mother always warned – spring! Beware the wild spring. I'm going.

SAM: Kiss?

GERTIE: Oh sharp. Sharp, sharp, sharp.

She offers her lips to him.

He kisses her lightly, not wildly.

The wind howls and only the sea is wild.

SCENE SIX

SAM's bed-sitter.

He's ill in bed. Caught cold by the sea.

GERTIE in a chair at his bedside.

He's just finishing a plate of soup she's made and brought to him.

GERTIE: The Scots swear by it. Broth. Scotch broth. My husband's mother taught me how to make it. *She* wasn't Scottish but her husband was. *(Beat.)* My husband's father. *(Beat.)* She was his second wife. *(Beat.)* My husband's stepmother. *(Beat.)* Don't try to work it out. *(Beat.)* The only thing she ever *did* teach me. Didn't rate me very high, my step-mother-in-law. Said I was the dullest thing on two legs.

He's finished the soup.

SAM: Great. Thanks.

GERTIE: *You* don't think I'm the dullest thing on two legs do you?

SAM: What's this full of foolishness you are?

GERTIE: Are you Caribbean-talking to me?

SAM: Me don't wan' no foolish conversation wi' you.

GERTIE: Me *what*?

SAM: Me tink time's come we talk de trut.

GERTIE: *(Attempting it.)* You're no capable of talking de trut, mun.

SAM: You'd make a rotten black woman.

GERTIE: So would you.

SAM: Jesus Christ! I ain't never been so ill.

GERTIE: Have you taken your temperature?

SAM: What with?

GERTIE: Funny you should ask. It so happens that here in my
 bag –

She draws out a thermometer.

Now, you know what you can do with this, don't you?

SAM: Under my tongue?

GERTIE: Not this thermometer.

SAM: Under my arm?

GERTIE: Not this thermometer.

SAM: You don't mean – ?

GERTIE: I do mean!

SAM: But that's rude.

GERTIE: And accurate.

SAM: You're corrupting me.

GERTIE: Do you want to live or die?

SAM: There's more than one way of dyin', ya know.

GERTIE: Oh sharp –

TOGETHER: – sharp, sharp, sharp.

SAM*: You* do it.

GERTIE: Not so likely. It does *not* befit our relationship.

SAM: What if you were a nurse?

GERTIE: Well I'm not a nurse. I'm an actress.

SAM: Act nurse to me.

GERTIE: Not even if you were Juliet in drag.

SAM: It could be your most rewarding role.

GERTIE: Will you stick this where it counts so's we can know how hot you are?

SAM: I don't need no thermometer up my arse to tell me how hot I am. I *know* how hot I am. I'm *very* hot. I'm so hot I'm burning underneath these blankets. *(Lifts them.)* Feel.

GERTIE: Sa-am!

> *She thrusts thermometer into his hand and discretely turns away.*
>
> *He runs a finger down her back. She shifts forward out of reach.*
>
> *Comic scene as he wriggles to find 'the entrance'.*

SAM: Oooh, it's cold. *(Wriggles.)* I can't find it. Where is it? I've lost it. *(Wriggles.)* Ah. *(Finds it. Pushes.)* Mmmmm. *(Beat.)* Nice.

GERTIE: That day out by the sea. You weren't dressed warmly enough.

SAM: Which is why I needed to be kissed –

GERTIE: Only twice.

SAM: – which is why I caught cold. Denied the warmth of your passion.

GERTIE: Passion is rare, to be offered sparingly.

SAM: To husbands.

GERTIE: That's right.

SAM: Surprised your mum ever let you get married.

GERTIE: On my wedding day I caught her looking dramatically out of the window –

SAM: Little drama-queen was she?

GERTIE: That was her! 'You all right, mum?' I asked. 'I'm all right' she replied. 'It's just that now you've left me my life is over and I don't think I'll be alive next year.'

SAM: Great send off.

GERTIE: She meant well.

SAM: Happy marriage was it?

GERTIE: Ups and downs.

SAM: What were the downs?

GERTIE: His secretary moving in.

SAM: I'm sorry.

GERTIE: Don't be sorry. She said she'd never been so well looked after.

SAM: Did you ever get happy again?

GERTIE: You're getting very personal.

SAM: What are friends for?

Pause, as she considers.

GERTIE: The last six months of Gerry dying were the happiest. Poor Gerry. Had to wait to die to be happy. He wanted to get back into theatre directing after running a TV company but no one wanted to know. Went cap-in-hand to theatres in the sticks – turned down! After being so famous, one of the early TV personalities – turned down.

SAM: Tough.

GERTIE: Very tough.

SAM: What did he do?

GERTIE: Opened a pub. I did the cooking.

SAM: Famous actress cooking in a pub?

GERTIE: I was given some of the best roles of the season and I cooked in between rehearsals.

SAM: Mrs Everybody were you?

GERTIE: One and a half years later he was dead. One year out of work, year and half running the pub – dead! And the six months nursing him in the hotel were the happiest.

SAM: Happiest? Nursing the dying?

GERTIE: Probably because I was needed! Needed to be part of a company, needed to be part of a family. Needed to be needed.

SAM: How could you play leading roles, look after Tom, cook pub food, and nurse a dying man for Christ's sake?

GERTIE: Piece of cake. Boring just being an actress.

SAM: You *do* see yourself as Mrs Everybody don't you?

GERTIE: That thermometer –

SAM: Mrs Ordinary Everybody!

GERTIE: – should be boiling by now.

SAM: It's called inverted snobbery.

GERTIE: Give!

> *Another comic scene as he pretends he can't find it.*

SAM: Oh! Where is it? Where'd I put it? I've lost it. Help! I've swallowed it.

> *She turns abruptly to him. He holds it up. She holds out her hand for it.*

SAM: *(Handing it to her.)* Cor! You're taking risks aren't you?

> *She peers.*

GERTIE: You've got a temperature all right. Hundred and one point one.

> *She goes off.*
>
> *Sound of tap running.*

(Voice off, bossy.) You'll stay in bed for a week. I'll bring you food and hot lemon drinks and you'll sweat it out. I'll change your sheets, wash your pyjamas, and bring you books to read. I'll also speak to the office to make sure you don't lose pay. You'll be better than new before you can say Ginger Rogers.

SAM: I thought it was Jack Robinson.

She returns with a wet flannel.

GERTIE: I don't know who Jack Robinson is.

SAM: I don't know who Ginger Rogers is.

GERTIE: I may be older but you're not *that* much younger. Here, lie still with this on your forehead.

He lies back. He's really very weak.

SAM: I'm grateful, Gertie.

GERTIE: Hush.

SAM: Serious now. I had a rotten mum. Not rotten, she just didn't know how to be a mum. Which is strange if you think about it. It's usually the black mums who know how to be mums while the black dads don't know how to be dads. But my dad's alright. Works as a ticket inspector on the Underground.

GERTIE: And your mum?

SAM: She really is dead. Only not from cancer. And there was no hundred thousand pounds either. *(Pause.)* Mmm! This is lovely.

GERTIE: The flannel is cooling.

SAM: It's not the flannel, it's being looked after.

GERTIE: Don't be maudlin.

SAM: What's 'maudlin'?

GERTIE: Saaaammmm…

SAM: Well, I reckon some of the best things in life are maudlin – like love, having babies, ice-cream, being looked after…

GERTIE: Hush, you'll tire yourself out.

SAM: Cor, I suddenly feel – whacked, weak. I've *never* felt so weak. I just want to sleep. Sink into the bed, close my eyes and sleep.

GERTIE: Then close your eyes and sleep, darling.

SAM: They're so heavy.

GERTIE: Don't fight it. Close them.

SAM: Couldn't keep them open if I wanted to.

GERTIE: Sleep.

SAM: It's the middle of the afternoon.

GERTIE: Sleep.

SAM: When I close my eyes…

GERTIE: Sleep.

SAM: Goodnight, Mrs Ordinary Everybody.

GERTIE: A car-park attendant indeed!

SCENE SEVEN

GERTIE's dressing room in half-light.

But first, off stage, GERTIE as Lady Macbeth. (Act 2. SCENE 2.)

GERTIE'S VOICE: '*That which hath made them drunk hath made me bold:*
What hath quench'd them hath given me fire: – Hark! Peace!
It was the owl that shriek'd, the fatal bellman
Which gives the stern'st good-night. He is about it.
The doors are open and the surfeited grooms
Do mock their charge with snores: I have drugg'd their possets,
That death and nature do contend about them,
Whether they live, or die.

Voice fades.

Silence.

Applause. Lights up in dressing room.

SAM enters backwards followed by a dazed GERTIE. She's in the nightdress of their last scene.

SAM: You were fantastic tonight. Fan-fucking-tastic.

GERTIE: I know it.

SAM: Best ever.

GERTIE: I know it, I know it.

SAM: Why? Out of nowhere. Just like that. Why?

GERTIE: I don't know.

SAM: I've never seen such an audience. They were –

GERTIE: – electrified. I know it.

SAM: Why does it happen?

GERTIE: I don't know.

SAM: *How* does it happen?

GERTIE: I don't know, I don't know.

SAM: You must know.

GERTIE: You're asking questions, Samson Martin, which touch on the deepest mysteries of life. Don't!

SAM: I want to know.

GERTIE: I don't want to think about it. Something like that happens you don't ask questions, you get down on your knees and you give thanks.

SAM: Then how do you know how to do it again?

GERTIE: You don't! And when you think you do, you fail.

SAM: Well, you don't do *nothing.* You don't go out with your fingers crossed.

GERTIE: You rehearse.

SAM: Yeah. We know all about rehearse, don't we? Actresses rehearse and rehearse and ask deeply serious questions and look deeply, deeply thoughtful – nothing! Zilch!

GERTIE: *(Insisting.)* You rehearse.

SAM: You're frightened to admit the truth aren't you, Mrs Everybody?

> *No response.*

Mrs Ordinary Everybody.

> *No response.*

Some people 'ave got it and some people ain't!

GERTIE: Haven't.

SAM: And you'd like to think that everybody's got it 'cos you like thinking we're all one happy family. But we ain't.

GERTIE: Aren't.

SAM: Some is and some isn't. Some 'ave and some 'aven't. Am I right, Mrs Everybody? Mrs Everybody! Mrs Ordinarybody! Mrs Ordinary Everybody. All that modesty stuff. *(Mocking.)* 'I don't know where it comes from. I just go out there and do it. It's not me, really. I want to thank the director and my designer and my husband who stood by me and the carpenter and –

GERTIE: – and God –

SAM: – and God –

GERTIE: – and the car-park attendant –

SAM: – inverted snobbery! You ain't just ordinary everybody. Your mum made mischief, you're Mrs Special Body. *You've* got it, *they* 'aven't.

GERTIE: Don't you talk to me about 'special' and 'who's got it' and 'who hasn't' Mr Car-park Attendant, Mr Wet-rag, Mr Window-wiper, Mr Wheel-changer!

SAM: I haven't got it!

GERTIE: That's right. You're black. I forgot. *(Beat.)* A car-park attendant indeed! Get off my back and go to college.

SAM: To do what?

GERTIE: How the hell should I know? All I know is I'd prefer you to use your intelligence on a tough professor instead of hitting poor little me over the head with it. I've had a great night. I'm the toast of the company. You should be showering me with care and loving kindness.

SAM: *(Contrite.)* Bloody hell. I'm sorry. After such a performance. Rotten of me. Sorry.

> *Pause.*

GERTIE: *(Calling to her dresser.)* Lottie? You can go, love. I'll chuck the nightdress into my own wash. See you tomorrow.

SAM: You roared like a bull.

GERTIE: How about 'raged like the possessed'?

SAM: How about 'delivered like a demon'?

GERTIE: How about 'shone like the sun'?

SAM: How about 'erupted like a volcano'?

GERTIE: How about 'flashed like a falling star'?

SAM: You mean 'shooting star'?

GERTIE: Do I?

> *Pause. Reflect on that.*

Stars have to fall some day.

SAM: Some do, some don't. Like some 'ave got it and some ain't. *(Beat.)* Haven't.

> *Phone rings. SAM answers it. Listens. Holds out phone to GERTIE.*

For you. Nanny.

> *She suddenly seems frightened.*

> *Doesn't take it. Cups her hand over receiver instead.*

GERTIE: What does she sound like?

SAM: *(Uncomprehending.)* What?

GERTIE: Her voice. What did it sound like? Light? Heavy?

SAM: I don't know. I didn't listen. Strict. Like nannies.

GERTIE: She's not a strict nanny. Oh God!

> *She moans, sits.*

SAM: What's happening?

> *She takes the phone.*

GERTIE: Nanny? *(Listens.)* Confirmed? *(Listens.)* I'm coming.

> *Blackout.*

SCENE EIGHT

TOM's bedside.

GERTIE there.

GERTIE: I'm sorry, Tom. Some things I could do for you, some I couldn't. Some things I can help, some I can't. But mum will look after you. That's what mums are for aren't they, to look after their children, be there, run around for them? And there's no doubt I run around for you. Got me running around all over the place haven't you, on the end of your little string? I shouldn't let you do it, you'll grow up spoilt and impossible. You're not very possible now, are you, poor ole fellow? God made you only half possible.

Wonder why he did that? Got tired half way did he? Do
you think he did that with most of us? Got tired half way?
Feels like it sometimes, that I'm only half made. It's all
right when I'm up there on the stage being wonderful and
loved and admired, but there's the rest of the time.

Still – the rest of the time is you, isn't it? Thank God for
you, Tom. Acting and looking after you go well together.
There's only half of you and only half of me which makes
a good fit I'd say. Wouldn't you? So don't close your eyes,
Tom, stay awake with me. I need you. To fit the other half.
You'll make him stay, won't you, God? I mean, I know
you work in mysterious ways, but don't be too mysterious.
Not all the time. I mean – give yourself a break, throw a
little light on things now and then, I've got to understand
something... Don't be mean about meaning, there's a good
God.

SCENE NINE

Rehearsal room.

GERTIE rehearsing Gertrude in Hamlet. (Act 3. Scene 4.)

SAM watching.

GERTIE: '*Alas, how is' with you,*
 That you do bend your eye on vacancy,
 And with th' incorporal air do hold discourse?
 Forth at your –

> *She's interrupted by 'the director'.*

Yes, James? *(Listens.)* Why do you want me to make a
question of the *whole* line? *(Listens.)* Yes, I know she's
bewildered but I think you'll get the right emotion if
you get the meaning first, and *I* think Gertrude is asking
Hamlet why he's talking to the air. 'Th' incorporeal air' is
what I should go for. *(Demonstrates.)* Hamlet asks her 'Alas
how is't with you?' She responds:

'*Alas, how ist with* **you**,
That you do bend your eye on vacancy,
And with th' incorporal air do hold discourse?'

Your way it's – well, listen:

> *Demonstrates, applying the questioning tone on each*
> *of the three lines.*

'*Alas, how is' with you,*
That you do bend your eye on vacancy,
And with th' incorporal air do hold discourse?'

I think it comes out too – heavy. But can I finish it please?
I don't think I've ever had a chance to deliver this speech
through to the end without you interrupting me.

> *The combination of her anguish over TOM dying and*
> *irritation with the director gives extra depth to her*
> *rendering of the passage.*
>
> *She delivers it as though asking TOM to 'sprinkle cool*
> *patience' and not look at death.*

Alas, how is' with you,
That you do bend your eye on vacancy,
And with th' incorporal air do hold discourse?
Forth at your eyes your spirits wildly peep,
And, as the sleeping soldiers in th' alarm,
Your bedded hair, like life in excrements,
Start up and stand an end. O gentle son,
Upon the heat and flame of thy distemper
Sprinkle cool patience. Whereon do you look?

> *It was moving. Waits for her note.*

Did you? Yes, well I'm feeling a little sad today, perhaps
that helps. *(Listens.)* Oh, nothing serious. Just one of those
days. It'll pass. *(Listens.)* What a strange question. *Every*
actor thinks there's more than one way to deliver a line.
(Pause.) But to tell you the truth, now you ask, I'm not
certain. I think, oh dear, I'm not sure I can say this, you'll

disagree violently, but I have this horrible suspicion there's probably only *one* right way to deliver a line and all the time we're struggling to find it – that one right way. And we think each time we do it differently, each time another actor is doing it differently, that we're giving a different 'interpretation'. But we're not. It's not really interpretation is it? We do it differently because we can't *help* doing it differently – we are each of us different and in our different ways we're struggling to find the one right way to deliver it, to get the line into focus. A bit like life – we struggle to find the one right way to live it, to get it in focus, get back to paradise. Never succeed of course. Paradise is unattainable and life's always out of focus, isn't it? But that doesn't stop us aiming for paradise, focus, the one right way. *(Pause.)* Can I tell you a story – perhaps it's time for a break?

SAM brings her a chair to sit on.

GERTIE may or may not sit on it.

I was at a dinner once, not theatre people but – others. A mixed crowd – writers, business people, media – and I happened to say to my neighbour at the dinner table just what I've said now, that there's probably only one right way to deliver a line. And this neighbour, a businessman, turned abruptly on me and said '*Well I think that's the biggest load of nonsense I've ever heard*'. Rude and abrupt. No discussion, just insult. It hurt I can tell you. So I shut up. Went silent. Sulked probably.

And the hostess could see something was wrong, so she asked what had happened. And the whole table went quiet and turned to us. Terrifying. But I thought: I'll try something out. And I told them. 'This man' I said, 'this gentleman on my right here, we were having a discussion about acting and I put it to him that there was probably only one right way to deliver a line, and he said –

She imitates an exaggeratedly apologetic man.

'well I think that's the biggest load of nonsense I've ever heard'. At which he protested, saying 'No, no! I didn't say it like that. I don't have a pathetic nature.' 'Oh, of course' I said, 'you said it like this – '

She imitates an exaggeratedly loud and aggressive man.

'Well I think that's the biggest load of nonsense I've ever heard'! At which he protested again. 'No, no! I didn't say it like that either. I don't have a a belligerent nature.' 'Oh, I'm sorry' I said. 'Do you mean there's only one right way you delivered your line?'

She allows this to sink in.

Despite the intensity of her anecdote her mind is elsewhere.

The 'director' is questioning her.

(Listening.) Yes, something *is* wrong. Tom is dying. Leukaemia. *(Listening.)* Yes – in *very* mysterious ways.

SCENE TEN

TOM's bedside.

GERTIE there.

GERTIE: *O gentle son, upon the heat and flame of thy distemper, sprinkle cool patience. Whereon do you look?*

Not at death, Tom. Don't take any notice of the Old Reaper. He's looking for ancients. Those who've lived a long life, those who are tired. Not you, Tom. You've got ages and ages and ages and ages. I've got plans for you. Plans you'll like. Travel to weird and wonderful places. Don't go from me, lovely boy. Behave, now. I don't want to be a lonely old woman.

SCENE ELEVEN

A crematorium.

Hum of people.

Music – Adagio from Mozart's string trio: Divertemento in E flat major.

GERTIE comforted by SAM.

GERTIE: I think I wanted to be a mother more than anything else. So many miscarriages. Thought the fault was mine, like I always think the fault was mine. Our doctor offered to test us. Gerry refused. So I went when I still had some of him inside me. She showed me what was under the microscope. Gerry's were flat out, exhausted, mine were up there dancing. *(Small laugh.)* Poor Gerry. I didn't tell him. We just adopted Tom. *(Pause.)* Oh Tom, Tom, Tom.

Pulls herself together.

Do you realise – if I evaporated at four in the morning I'd not leave a hole in anyone's life?

SAM: I'd –

GERTIE: Don't say *you'd* miss me. And if you did you'd soon get over it.

SAM: What about –

GERTIE: What about no one! There's no one. You blacks and the Jews have hundreds of aunts and cousins all over the place. I've got no one.

Do you know, when my dad died he said to Gerry 'don't let mum swallow up Gertie anymore'. Poor dad. I only got to know anyone was there in his last months. It's always the last months. I didn't even know what his politics were? I just knew he used to stand up at night in the living room when the National Anthem played on tele. *(Pause.)* What made me think of that suddenly? This solemn atmosphere

I suppose. *(Pause.)* Poor Gerry. Glad he's not alive for this death.

> *They share a smile.*

SAM: Want to hold my hand?

GERTIE: What, with all that lot watching?

SAM: They'll understand.

GERTIE: They won't! But who cares. Just for a minute.

> *He holds out his hand and she takes it.*

Oh, I'll recover. We all do. Survive and recover. Problem with me is I feel guilty about it. Everything pains me, even surviving. Terrible affliction.

> *Suddenly, as though struck with divine revelation, but really she's flipped.*

He's alive. Tom's not dead, he's alive. I know it.

SAM: Gertie, easy now.

GERTIE: *(Shouting to 'Funeral Director'.)* Open his coffin!

SAM: Gertie, don't do this.

GERTIE: I know he's still alive. I want his coffin opened.

SAM: You're upset, Gertie.

GERTIE: I feel it. I want his coffin opened.

SAM: It's a loss, Gertie, we know, and you're probably more shocked than you realised...

GERTIE: I want his coffin opened.

SAM: Gertie! Be sensible! Tom's been screwed down four days now. He can't be alive.

GERTIE: And what if he is?

> *She waits for that awful possibility to sink in.*

What, what if he is? My boy. Depending on me. My son, waiting for his mother to rescue him? My child. What if he is?

SAM: It's just not possible, Gertie. It doesn't make sense.

GERTIE: And how will I feel for the rest of my life if I don't make certain?

> *She leaves.*
>
> *SAM sinks to his knees on to the hassock.*
>
> *Nothing but the low hum of people and the music.*
>
> *A drained GERTIE returns, joins SAM on her knees.*

GERTIE: I don't believe in God. Why am I on my knees?

SAM: You're saying goodbye, ent you.

> *She is weeping.*
>
> *Fade.*
>
> *End of Act One.*

Act Two

SCENE ONE

Fifteen years have passed.

GERTIE, with her back to us, is performing 'Lear's' Fool to an unseen audience.

FOOL: '*This is a brave night to cool a courtezan –*
I'll speak a prophecy ere I go.
When priests are more in word than matter;
When brewers mar their malt with water;
When –

> *She dries.*

GERTIE: Yes?

PROMPT: '*When nobles are their tailors' tutors –* '

FOOL: '*When nobles are their tailors' tutors;*
No heretics burn'd, but wenches' suitors;
When every case in law is right;
When –

GERTIE: Yes?

PROMPT: '*No squire in debt –*

FOOL: '*No squire in debt, nor no poor knight;*
When –

GERTIE: Yes?

PROMPT: '*When slanders do not live in tongues –* '

FOOL: '*When slanders do not live in tongues –*

> *She dries again. Freezes.*
>
> *She turns to face us –*
>
> *– terror-struck.*

SCENE TWO

GERTIE's dressing room.

She sits before her mirror, trembling violently.

She attempts many things to control herself. A drink – it spills. A cigarette – she coughs.

GERTIE: *(To her dresser.)* No, I'm all right, Lottie. You can go. Yes. I'm sure.

> *Deep breathing – coughs even more.*

I am not going to cry. I *am* not.

> *Begins to wipe off make-up.*

'You look so ugly when you cry.'

> *The remains of prettiness linger about her eyes.*

> *KENNEDY, a black company manager of around thirty, enters with a tray of food kept warm by a silver hood; a pot of tea and its accoutrements.*

> *He pours out tea. Hands her a cup. It rattles in her hand. He holds her firm. As he's holding –*

GERTIE: When I was three years old I announced 'I, Gertrude Matthews, am going to be a fairy.'

KENNEDY: Ambitious from the word go.

GERTIE: Double pneumonia at two. Had to be taught to walk again. Doctor advised dancing lessons. Good exercise. A year later I announced 'I, Gertrude Matthews, am going to be a fairy'.

KENNEDY: Can I let go now?

GERTIE: You can try.

> *He lets go. The trembling recommences. He takes hold again.*

At eight I started ballet lessons with a famous ballet mistress who told me I walked like a crab. 'You walk like

a crab, I hope you don't dance like one.' Insults! They've
never stopped.

KENNEDY: Tell me when I can let go.

GERTIE: 'Don't you go thinking *you've* got talent, Gertie' my
mum used to say. 'It's just God's gift.'

KENNEDY: I'm letting go.

GERTIE: She was probably right.

KENNEDY: You do talk nonsense don't you?

He lets go.

GERTIE: There! You see? Another insult.

Hands trembling again.

KENNEDY: *(Again taking hold.)* Maybe you invite them.

GERTIE: I married a man whose step-mother told me I was the
dullest thing on two legs. Did I invite that?

KENNEDY: Jealousy.

GERTIE: 'Gertie hasn't got looks but she's got character.' Did I
invite that?

KENNEDY: She said you had character.

GERTIE: 'If only you smiled like the Harmer girl. Renee
Harmer is *so* pretty. You watch that Harmer girl, *she'll* go
places.'

KENNEDY: I'm letting go.

He does so.

There. Better.

GERTIE: I learned that it *was* possible to do more than one's
best, but it was never quite good enough for my mum.

She drinks. Puts down cup, exhausted.

GERTIE: My understudy's good isn't she, Mr Phillips?

KENNEDY: Very good. Why do you ask?

> *GERTIE has learned how to protect her vulnerability with bawdy humour.*

GERTIE: *(Evading an answer.)* Why don't we go out for dinner tonight?

KENNEDY: Gertie, will you stop making passes at me?

GERTIE: Why should I? The spring is coming. I feel wild stirrings.

KENNEDY: Here, I've bought you half a bottle of the best Bordeaux.

GERTIE: *(Cod slav accent.)* I want your body.

KENNEDY: *(Cod slav accent.)* Well I don't want your's.

> *She pulls open her dressing gown, flashing her breasts.*

GERTIE: You sure, Mr Phillips?

KENNEDY: They're very nice, yes, now put them away and eat your steak.

GERTIE: If you don't want my body why do you look after me, buy me expensive wine, hang around as though I were a bitch on heat?

KENNEDY: Because as company manager I'm paid to look after you, and because you're a great actress from whom I learn something each night.

GERTIE: Like how to dry?

KENNEDY: Every actor dries at least once in their life.

GERTIE: But not twice a week. Look –

> *She holds out her shaking hand.*

can you tremble like that?

KENNEDY: Of course I can.

> *He holds out his hand. It trembles.*

GERTIE: You're just acting.

> *Drinks deeply.*

'Just acting'. Are you aware, Mr Phillips, that society normally uses the name of our profession as a term of abuse? 'Oh ignore her, she's just acting!' Are you aware, Mr Phillips, that every night I go out there in front of an audience and pretend to be who I am not? Are you aware, Mr Phillips, that if I did that in public-life I'd be shunned, vilified, called a humbug, a fraud, a sham, a fake, a liar, but up there, made-up, lights bright, someone else's words of wit and brilliance, I can dissemble to my heart's content, it's acceptable, no one gives a toss. What is despised in a person *off* stage I am deceiving an audience to praise *on* stage. And the more convincingly I deceive the more they praise. They even pay for it. Are you aware of all that, Mr Phillips? Audacious, huh? What other profession do you know where the professional exposes herself to the ridicule of disbelief, the ignominy of dismissal, the humiliation of being seen through, and makes that her raison d'étre, her justification for existing, eh? What other profession?

> *Her make-up is off. Her face is 'naked'. She pulls her hair to stick up, defiantly making herself unattractive.*

Come to bed. I have such delights to offer you.

> *GERTIE from here on will change, make up, occasionally cut her food and feed it to KENNEDY.*

> *He loves her sufficiently to ride her flippancy and address her serious side.*

KENNEDY: You are not asking your audience to praise your acting...

GERTIE: You could demand whatever you desired.

KENNEDY: You are not saying to an audience 'look at me aren't I a clever actor'.

GERTIE: Even lie on top if you like.

KENNEDY: Be serious! You miss the point of acting.

GERTIE: Oh, I do, do I? After twenty-five years of giving my all, I miss the point of all I gave?

She goes off to shower conversing from there.

KENNEDY: You're asking an audience to listen, think and feel about what it is your *character* says, thinks and feels.

GERTIE: Through an actor!

KENNEDY: Yes. *Through* an actor. But the theatre is not *about* actors any more than medicine is about doctors. Medicine is about saving life, acting is about representing life.

GERTIE: Artificially!

KENNEDY: Everything human beings do, except bodily functions like eating, sleeping and you-know-what –

GERTIE: *(Lasciviously.)* Oh yes, I do, I do, I do know what –

KENNEDY: – everything other than the above mentioned could be called artificial. Words, signs, songs, dance – they're all artifacts for representing selections from the real thing, which is life itself.

GERTIE: Oh, sharp! Sharp, sharp and sexy.

KENNEDY: I've never thought it either useful or helpful to describe what we do as acting.

GERTIE: A thinking man is so sexy!

KENNEDY: We represent. We employ a skill, a skill to represent selections in the life of –

GERTIE: – a Fool!

GERTIE reappears in a bathrobe.

Pa-poum!

Sits before mirror to make-up.

GERTIE: Why do I dry as Lear's Fool? What is there about that speech?

KENNEDY: Lists! The speech is a list. Meaning – drives, pulls you along. In a list it's easy to get lost.

GERTIE: It's not just the drying, it's the fearing. And it's not just the fearing, it's the fear of fearing. It's the putting yourself up there when the 'believe-in-me' is gone. Everything goes out of your head. Your body is paralysed. Terror! It's to do with being caught out. If you dry then everybody suddenly knows you've been 'just acting'. Blood drains from you and in its place shame seeps like poison through your whole system. I've often stood in the wings and thought – I'm not going out there. I can't do that show again tonight. And I've wanted to lock myself in the dressing room. And I think – when will that day come, locking myself in – when is it going to be me?

Long pause. Mood changing.

Ha! There was this actor who'd made up a set of seven lines for when *he* dried in a Shakespeare role.

'Aye, my Lord, yonder Hereford cometh
And Shrewsbury too. And York hath mounted
And will shortly come. Behold is yonder
Basingstoke your favourite forsooth
And Cornwall calls thee home to rest.
Look, sire, Somerset and Dorset too
And Surrey, aye, and Buckingham…

By which time he'd either remembered the lines or his colleagues had fed him.

Both are convulsed.

KENNEDY: The counties, thank God for the English counties.

GERTIE: 'Look, sire, Somerset and Dorset too…'

KENNEDY: 'And Surrey, aye, and Buckingham…' *(Laughter.)*

GERTIE: They could be made to fit anything.

KENNEDY: Not *any*thing, surely. Histories, maybe, but what if he dried in Romeo and Juliet?

GERTIE: 'Romeo, Romeo –' *(Beat.)* ' – and Somerset and Dorset too…'

KENNEDY: 'And Surrey, aye, and Buckingham…'

They have difficulty stemming their laughter.

GERTIE: Tell me about your mum for a change.

KENNEDY: My mum? Married at seventeen, had five children, and when the youngest was fourteen said goodbye to us all and went off with a dark stranger. It was as if she'd just been given the charge of us for a short while until the time came to give us back. Though who to, we never found out. She rings one of us now and then but we don't see much of her. Strange lady. Laughed at everything and seemed to understand nothing. When we meet she looks at us as though she's trying to remember who we are.

GERTIE: What about poor old dad?

KENNEDY: Poor old dad is a very bewildered, incompetent brick-layer who works non-stop for builders with no standards. His wife going off with a dark stranger bewildered him; his children's ability to thrive and survive without either of them bewilders him; and the builders who continue to employ him bewilder him.

GERTIE: You feel close to your people?

KENNEDY: My *what*?

GERTIE: People! I said 'people'. *(To an imaginary neighbour.)* I did say 'people', didn't I?

KENNEDY: *(Sardonically.)* Which 'people'? My family 'people' or my black 'people'?

GERTIE: Oh dear. Have I asked the wrong question? Soorreeee!

KENNEDY: I once got into a fight at school defending a white boy against the overwhelming odds of three black boys who turned on me and screamed 'Where are your roots, black boy? Don'tcha know where you belong? Roots, man, roots! Remember your roots!' To which I replied 'My roots are anywhere intelligence is'. Having said which they laid me out flat as a slab for the dead.

GERTIE: Complicated.

KENNEDY: Complicated.

GERTIE: So from whence your desire to act?

KENNEDY: Don't know. My Dominican great-grandfather is purported to have been seduced by a runaway can-can dancer who'd pinched her ageing lover's silver.

GERTIE: Say that again.

KENNEDY: My Dominican great-grandfather is purported to have been seduced by a runaway can-can dancer who'd pinched her ageing lover's silver.

GERTIE: Complicated.

KENNEDY: Complicated.

She's provocatively putting on her grip stockings.

GERTIE: Nice legs?

KENNEDY: Gorgeous.

GERTIE: Yours if you play your cards right.

He parries her bawdiness as usual.

KENNEDY: Gertie –

GERTIE: Sounds ominous.

KENNEDY: – do you think I have a talent for acting?

Long pause.

You paused too long. I have no talent for acting.

GERTIE: It's not that you have no talent for acting, it's that…
well…you act as though you don't really want to.

KENNEDY: It shows?

GERTIE: Know what I think?

KENNEDY: I didn't think it showed.

GERTIE: I think you should apply to run a theatre.

KENNEDY: And yet I desperately want to act.

GERTIE: Become a producer!

KENNEDY: Or perhaps I should be directing. Or writing. Or –

GERTIE: Producers have the power.

KENNEDY: I've thought about it.

GERTIE: Don't think, do!

KENNEDY: It so happens I'm good with money.

GERTIE: See! Not a qualification for acting.

KENNEDY: I actually do understand money.

GERTIE: So go out and get rich and make me your mistress.

KENNEDY: I'll confess something –

GERTIE: – or one of them!

KENNEDY: – I've actually made money. I bought a house
when I was 24, got a 90% mortgage, sold it in the last of
the boom years, made a killing and invested.

GERTIE: And lost?

KENNEDY: No. I'm ashamed to admit it, but I invested wisely.

GERTIE: Good Lor! But how did you know? From where? I
mean…what…?

KENNEDY: I have this gift. I can make money reproduce itself. I've always had it. Since school days. I traded. In anything. Buy from one boy and sell to another. No one knew. I always had money and no one knew how. Used to think I stole.

Sometimes when I close my eyes the language of finance floats before me. I feel as though I'm engaged with something supremely wicked, like being with a marvellous whore. Everything is possible. 'Dividend'. 'Charge account'. 'Money supply'. 'White knight'. 'Opening price'. 'Elastic currency'. 'Liquidity'. 'Open mouth operations'. 'Risk capital'. 'Placing'. 'Over night money'. 'Order'. 'Tender'. 'Yield'. A world vibrating with challenge, stimulating the imagination, releasing energies. To buy with one hand and sell with the other, to know what to buy and when to sell, to judge what the market needs, the price it can take.

And other times when I close my eyes the language of poetry floats before me.

And on the pedestal these words appear:
'My name is Ozymandias, king of kings;
Look on my works, ye Mighty, and despair!'
Nothing beside remains. Round the decay
Of that colossal wreck, boundless and bare
The lone and level sands stretch far away.

I'm a torn man, Gertie – artist or trader?

GERTIE: That's why I love you, you've got problems!

KENNEDY: Artist or mammon?

GERTIE: Go for mammon, more user-friendly.

KENNEDY: Why is it, do you suppose?

GERTIE: Why is it what do I suppose?

KENNEDY: Why is it that people want to be involved in the arts?

GERTIE: Glamour!

KENNEDY: I think it's God.

GERTIE: God?

KENNEDY: Being an artist, people feel, is like being in touch with the divine.

GERTIE: Being an artist is blood, sweat and tears.

KENNEDY: It's so difficult getting you to be serious.

GERTIE: Blood, sweat and tears is very serious.

KENNEDY: We all know about blood, sweat and tears, but when they've been spent, if you've made it come together – the novel, the painting, the symphony, the poem, the play – blessed! By God! Touched. By the divine! But money? Mammon?

GERTIE: I find money very thrilling.

KENNEDY: Me too. Thrilling. But a work of art – to assemble the beautiful parts of a work of art…ah!

GERTIE: Do you realise you burn when you're animated?

KENNEDY: Who got the deepest satisfaction from life, Masaccio who first gave perspective to painting, or the Medici who commissioned paintings?

GERTIE: Your eyes glow.

KENNEDY: Mozart or his patrons?

GERTIE: All fiery.

KENNEDY: Problem is – some of us have got it and some of us haven't.

GERTIE: Good God! Sam!

KENNEDY: Sam?

GERTIE: There used to be a young lad worked as a car-park attendant here. Samson Martin, he used to say that. 'Some's got it, and some ain't'.

KENNEDY: And did he have it?

GERTIE: What he had is the same as what you have – an identity crisis. Thought he was born to be a car-park attendant.

KENNEDY: Like I think I'm born to be an artist.

GERTIE: Like I don't know whether I'm coming or going.

Long pause.

KENNEDY: Eat your food.

GERTIE: Ah, food. Now, if you really want to know and understand everything about me, and you *do* want to know and understand everything about me don't you, Mr Phillips, because that's the only way you'll get me into bed, and I respect you for it, you don't rush a girl, I can see that – so if you really want to know and understand me – watch me eat.

She removes the covering hood.

Have you ever watched me eat?

KENNEDY: I prefer listening to you.

GERTIE: Love food, hate eating it. The act of cutting things up on a plate – how do you do it without it sliding off the edge? How do you push potatoes and beans with a knife on to a fork without them falling? And when you succeed and you feel safe enough to raise them to your mouth, how do you make sure they stay there? That's my real terror, food dropping off my fork, back onto the plate, splashing the hostess's best tablecloth, or my best dress. So I lower my face to the plate which I know is wrong, you're supposed to raise your food to your mouth, I know it, and sometimes I try, surreptitiously, which is impossible because by this time I know everyone is looking at me so I get embarrassed, and hover, and my face goes down and my fork comes up, a compromise, which doesn't work because my mouth is never ever where my fork imagines it is. I once pronged the back of my throat! You wouldn't think it possible would you? An anxious face went down too far and an eager fork came up too high. Aaarrrgghh!

Feigns strangulation.

Eating is an agony with only one other person, at a dinner table it's a nightmare.

Pause.

I'm glad you asked why I'm afflicted thus.

KENNEDY: Why are you afflicted thus, Gertrude?

GERTIE: Because, Mr Phillips, although I keep baldly asking you to impale yourself upon me I am, deep deep down where it counts, a very shy and tortured woman who feels she has to apologise for the air she breaths.

Pause.

I'm glad you asked me why I'm afflicted thus.

KENNEDY: Why are you afflicted thus, Gertrude?

GERTIE: Because, Mr Phillips, of mum –

KENNEDY: Ah, mum.

GERTIE: – who I idolised out of all proportion until I saw she had feet of clay and then I just stopped liking her. And when I stopped liking her I lost her. Like a bereavement. My fault, really, for making her a saint. We fall in love with images *we* make of ourselves and of other people. It's never really what we are or what they really are, is it?

KENNEDY: There must have been something lovable about her? Every mother has something lovable about them.

GERTIE: Lovable? She used to polish the window-ledges outside the house. Painted them glossy white then polished them. *(Pause.)* Taught me to stand on my head in the kitchen. *(Pause.)* She wanted to ride a motor-bike. *(Pause.)* She wanted to travel. *(Pause.)* She loved sherbet dabs and I loved it that my mum was a friend who loved sherbet dabs… Lovable? Yes. She was…

> *Offers her back to him, a wordless request to button-up her blouse.*

> *He does so. With her back still to him he asks:*

KENNEDY: What would you say is the most important tenet of the craft of acting?

GERTIE: Meaning. No question. Get the meaning right and the right emotion follows.

> *She turns to him. Dressed and made-up she looks beautiful but – terrified.*

Would you hold me, please?

> *He takes her in his arms, comfortingly.*

> *She clings.*

SCENE THREE

> *GERTIE's dining room, weeks later.*

> *She's at breakfast in a morning gown.*

> *Tea from a pot, toast and marmalade.*

> *Radio 3 music – the lively end of the first movement of Ravel's String Quartet in F. Major.*

> *Phone rings. Turns down radio before lifting receiver.*

GERTIE: *(Listening.)* Where are you? *(Listening.)* Up the road? That doesn't give me much time to undress. *(Listening.)* Problems? *You've* got problems? *(Listening.)* No no of course I don't mind. I'll get rid of my lovers, put on Radio 3, light a candle, pretend it's midnight instead of eight-thirty in the morning, and feed you. See ya.

> *By which time the second 'bubbly' movement of the quartet has commenced. Turns up radio.*

That's better.

> *The music tempts her to dance. She can't resist and flows around freestyle, expertly.*

'You look like a crab, I hope you don't dance like one.'

> *Door bell rings.*

'Up the road'?

> *She moves to open the door, repeating –*

'Up the road? Up the road? Up the road?'

> *She returns with KENNEDY.*

GERTIE: 'Up the road?'

KENNEDY: Round the corner then.

GERTIE: Didn't give me time to finish my morning dance.

KENNEDY: Morning dance?

GERTIE: I have tea, toast and marmalade, and dance every morning.

KENNEDY: I don't believe you.

GERTIE: You're quite right not to believe me. I *should* dance every morning. Come to bed with me? A quickie before we solve your problems and go to rehearsals?

KENNEDY: You're shameless.

GERTIE: Only with you. Only with you.

KENNEDY: Why do you do it?

GERTIE: Lust after you?

KENNEDY: Be sensible, Gertie.

GERTIE: At eight forty-five in the morning?

KENNEDY: Acting – why do you do it?

GERTIE: Is *that* your problem? Still agonizing between art and mammon?

KENNEDY: Crisis of identity, remember?

GERTIE: Most people are still coughing their way into the world at this time of the morning and you're agonizing between art and mammon?

KENNEDY: Did you say you'd feed me?

She senses something in his evasions.

GERTIE: Tea? Toast? Marmalade? Coffee?

He serves himself.

GERTIE: Don't you *ever* want to be looked after?

KENNEDY: All the men in my family hang around waiting to be looked after. I'm determined to depend on no one.

GERTIE: So why come to me with your problems?

KENNEDY: My physical being I'm in control of –

GERTIE: Don't I know it!

KENNEDY: – it's my soul that's in need. Acting – why?

GERTIE: Naked ambition.

KENNEDY: Don't believe you. That's only part of it.

GERTIE: A wish to be someone else.

KENNEDY: Don't believe you. That's only part of it.

GERTIE: Admiration, accolades, achievement.

KENNEDY: More. That's only part of it.

GERTIE: Power.

KENNEDY: Ah!

GERTIE: The power to control an audience, to manipulate them. To stir, to move, to thrill them. Come to bed!

KENNEDY: Getting believable.

GERTIE: The power to break their grip on what they imagine is reality and confront them with another reality. Come to bed!

KENNEDY: Keep going.

GERTIE: I've made audiences gasp. It's intoxicating. Like making a man come inside you.

KENNEDY: You are vivid at an early hour.

GERTIE: It's not the hour, it's my age. I can be vivid when I like. Come to bed!

KENNEDY: So acting is conquest for you?

GERTIE: Conquest, yes. Every actor is a Don Juan. Each night you seduce another audience. 'Love me' you tell them. 'Listen to me, love me, come to bed with me.'

KENNEDY: What about the craft, the skill?

GERTIE: That's the least you expect of a professional. Like telling a carpenter he handles his tools expertly. Fine! We should hope so! But what's the chair like? Like telling a playwright he writes good dialogue. Fine! We should hope so. But has the play any substance? Come to bed!

KENNEDY: So, you don't think I should pursue acting?

GERTIE: No. I think you should pursue me.

KENNEDY: I'm trying to map out the rest of my life, Gertie. Help me.

GERTIE: Come to bed, I'll help you.

> *He sighs.*

Don't take up acting. Every morning you'll wake up thinking is this the 'use by date'.

KENNEDY: *I'm* too young for that.

GERTIE: Then try this for size – rejection.

KENNEDY: Ah, rejection.

GERTIE: That's the killer. Coping with rejection. To be turned down for a part makes you feel unworthy to be alive – could you take that? 'Too old, too young, too short, too pretty, too good, not good enough, too experienced, not experienced enough.' Still want to be an actor? If they've seen you playing Shakespeare you don't get the Cockney part; if they see you in the Cockney part you don't get the countess. 'Oh, you're a comedienne!' 'Oh, you're a tragedienne!' Still want to be an actor? And then there are those interviews when the director tells you 'you could play this part with your hands tied behind your back' and you go home elated, and a month passes and you bump into a chum in the supermarket and ask her what she's doing and she tells you 'I'm rather excited actually, I'm doing ...' and she lets you know she's got the job you've been waiting a month to hear about and you suddenly feel like a cartload of cattle. Still want to be an actor?

KENNEDY: God, Gertie, you're desirable when you're angry.

GERTIE: There's women would hit you over the head for saying that but I love it. Tell me I'm desirable and I'll burn up on stage. There are two kinds of bad performance: one – due to no talent; two – due to no sex. If a good actor is having an off night you can bet your bottom dollar her lover's gone off her. When I was desired I was dynamite in performance. Tell me I'm not desirable and I enter stage right like lead. Ambition slinks off into the wings. I'm a dead lump. D-E-A-D, dead.

KENNEDY: L-U-M-P, lump!

GERTIE: Still want to be an actor?

KENNEDY: You telling me I'm not desirable?

GERTIE: Are you crazy? In lights: 'Kennedy Phillips. Nightly turn-on.'

KENNEDY: How often do you think you get it right?

GERTIE: What are we talking about here, the bed or the boards? Laid or stage?

KENNEDY: Stage, Gertie, stage.

GERTIE: Never, probably. And it's for sure mum's fault. Because I thought she was God I had to get everything right for her, and because directors are also God I feel I have to get everything right for them. Terrifies me. The figure who always expects you to get it right terrifies me so I get it wrong. And even when I get it right I'm not there. (Beat.) There! See what I mean? I always think I'm not there when I get it right. Perhaps it's the contrary, perhaps when I get it right I *am* there, it really *is* me getting it right. I always say I'm not there because I'm my mother saying 'You can't *really* be that good, not Gertie Matthews from Palmers Green.'

KENNEDY: Gertie –

> *She interrupts him with a violence in sharp contrast to her levity.*

GERTIE: I *know* what you're going to say.

> *Long pause.*

The company is not going to renew my contract.

KENNEDY: The Company is not going to renew your contract.

GERTIE: And they asked *you* to tell me?

KENNEDY: They knew we were close.

GERTIE: You? A company fucking manager? After twenty-five years on the fucking boards, taking shit from mediocrities a quarter my age, after stepping back for the young, after endless charities, prizes, accolades and thirty-five books of rave reviews, no director in that vast company has the courage to come himself and tell me personally 'Gertie stay home'?

KENNEDY: I'm sorry Gertie.

GERTIE: My God, Mr Phillips, you orchestrated your little errand with cunning.

KENNEDY: Delicacy.

GERTIE: 'Identity fucking crisis! Engage my sympathy, get me shooting my mouth off imagining I was *the* authority on acting and then give me my cards.

KENNEDY: I wanted you to remember how good you are.

GERTIE: Oh I knew what you were *doing*, Mr Phillips. Doesn't work, though. All confidence flees.

KENNEDY: Not forever, Gertie. You're a very special actress.

GERTIE: Rejection is rejection.

KENNEDY: They're shits.

GERTIE: Can't you hear them? Chinese whispers through the profession. 'Heard about Gertie? Having trouble with the wordies. Can't learn the lines.' Those I call the Green Room Brigade.

KENNEDY: Shits!

GERTIE: Oh go to rehearsals! Before you came I was a queen, dancing on air. Now I'm a cartload of cattle.

> *She is changed utterly. Part of a company – she was confident, full of bravado; deprived of a base – she deflates.*

'Don't you go thinking you've got talent, Gertie, it's just God's gift.'

KENNEDY: Gertie –

GERTIE: She was a killer.

KENNEDY: Gertie –

GERTIE: A killer!

KENNEDY: Can I –

GERTIE: Power! That's what my mum was interested in, power! Over people's lives. She treated dad like muck. Muck! He knew all about her but he adored her so she got away with it. Beyond the pale she was for him, even after she discovered drink and oh, did my mother discover drink! No stopping her manipulations then. Want to know why I dry? Because the killer still manipulates me from the grave. 'Don't you go thinking you've got talent, Gertie. It's just God's gift.' God? She didn't give a toss about God. Just made people love her and trust her so's that God-like she could control them.

But not the clever ones. Not our friends. Au pairs? Chambermaids? Had them eating out of her hand – they were inferior, see, she could control *them*. But not our friends. She went silent in front of *their* conversation. Anything she didn't understand intimidated her, so then she'd fuss around and do domestic and 'sensible' things and usually wreck our evenings.

And why do you think she sucked sherbet dabs with me, lovable ole mum? Not because she liked sherbet dabs, no! She sucked sherbet dabs with me like a 10 year old in order to be my friend. Partner 'gainst dad, see. 'Buy them at the corner shop, we'll eat them in the kitchen. Ssh! Our secret. Don't tell daddy.' 'Let's go to the cinema. After school. Every Wednesday. Ssh! Our secret. Don't tell daddy.' What a friend, I thought. She understood about sweets and movies on a school-day. 'Ssh! Our secret! Don't tell daddy.' Lovable? Killer!

And I lived in terror with all that nonsense for years and years till I was pock-marked with don'ts and guilts and confused messages sending me all over the place.

You know the season she hated most? Spring! A time
of growing, stirrings, wild winds. Hated it! Oh, she was
dangerous alright. One of the wasted women of the world
and there's nothing more dangerous than a wasted woman.
Killer! 'Don't tell daddy! Ssh! Our secret. Don't tell daddy!'
And then I discovered I loved him. Loved him! But too
late. Now that's a real guilt. I earned that one. Not like the
others which I had chained to me. Killer! I can't believe I
allowed all her malevolent nonsense to rule my life. Killer!
Killer, killer, killer!

KENNEDY: Gertie, can I say something?

GERTIE: So who can blame you for rejecting me...

KENNEDY: I get my holidays in two weeks time.

GERTIE: Or the company...

KENNEDY: Let's go somewhere.

GERTIE: Black kid, white grandmother?

KENNEDY: Friends.

GERTIE: Why?

KENNEDY: Why what?

GERTIE: Go somewhere.

KENNEDY: To take stock.

GERTIE: Reassess talents?

KENNEDY: No, replenish spirits.

GERTIE: Re-evaluate strengths?

KENNEDY: No, recharge batteries.

GERTIE: Reconsider my life?

KENNEDY: No. Your life is considered, it's just bruised, needs
to recover.

GERTIE: What did you have in mind, fellah?

KENNEDY: I cut this article out of a newspaper some time ago thinking I might need it one day. Look – Weekends For Lovers.

GERTIE: Thought you said 'friends'?

KENNEDY: No reason why friends shouldn't enjoy the same romantic settings as lovers. We'll take separate rooms and dine by candle-light. Look – Bell Hotel, Charlbury. *(Reading.) 'Lies on a rail link to Paddington, but you'll need a car if you plan on exploring the surrounding towns and villages such as Woodstock, Chipping Norton, Moreton in the Marsh...* Or how about a castle? *'Lumley Castle', County Durham...genuine thirteenth-century fortress.'* Protect us from the barbarians.

> *But GERTIE is weeping. He takes her in his arms.*

GERTIE: I tried to give up, honest I did. I didn't want to be just an actress, it didn't seem enough. Too frivolous. So I tried to give it up and find a way to make my life liveable by having a family. But I couldn't even keep an adopted son alive. Christ! Is there any further down to go? Oh, God! God! God! I hate crying. I absolutely hate women who cry.

> *He holds her tighter. We've seen them in this embrace before.*

KENNEDY: We must stop meeting like this.

> *Which makes her smile. He sits her down.*

I don't think you look ugly when you cry.

GERTIE: You don't really want to be an actor, do you?

KENNEDY: Not really.

GERTIE: Nor a company manager.

KENNEDY: Nor that.

GERTIE: So where's your crisis of identity? Give me a big crisis of identity. I need someone else's problem to think about so's I don't have to think about mine. I hate thinking about me. They say actors are self-centred and it may be true, but the last thing I want to do is think about me. Me, me, me! Me! Me! Me! Me! Me! Me! Me!

He clamps her mouth.

She's on the verge of hysterics.

KENNEDY: Come away with me to my castle in Durham and we'll talk about crisis of identity.

GERTIE: It's a unique relationship we have.

KENNEDY: All relationships are unique. Coming?

GERTIE: Can I suggest somewhere else?

SCENE FOUR

The beach – as Act 1 SCENE 5.

No high winds. Only the sound of the sea.

It's a gentle, sunny, warm, spring day.

GERTIE appears on the rock. She stands, remembering. Delivers the first and last line in recollection rather than performance.

GERTIE: '*Blow, winds and crack your cheeks! rage! blow! ... All germens spill at once, that make ungrateful man...*'

She begins to do the tai chi movements.

KENNEDY appears below. Watches her a while, then –

KENNEDY: You made love here?

GERTIE: *(Continuing t'ai chi.)* No. In my dressing room. And only once. A sort of sad consolation I permitted myself for losing an only child. Took a black boy in my arms to whiten my black despair. Wrap your racial sensibilities around that.

KENNEDY: I've already told you, I don't have them. My sensibilities are where intelligence resides.

Pause.

GERTIE: It was good of you to think of a break. It's helped.

KENNEDY: What happened to Sam?

GERTIE: I bullied him to college. He became a physiotherapist.

KENNEDY: He taught you tai chi?

GERTIE: Yes. Used to call me Mrs Everybody, Mrs Ordinary Everybody. Attacked me for trying to pretend I was more than an actress.

KENNEDY helps her to descend rock.

We sat there – I drank brandy he drank a Coke.

KENNEDY: *That* young?

Long pause.

The word 'young' sets off a train of thought.

GERTIE: Are you aware, Mr Phillips, how full the world is of lonely women? I could list you a dozen I know. Right now. All young to middle-aged. Professional or capable, single, with children, full of affection, lively, bursting to give and give and give. Lonely. Not for friendship but for love.

Why should that be do you think? I've never been able to fathom it out. Too fussy? Sexless? Too intelligent? Too demanding? Do we overwhelm? Give out the wrong smells? Do we carry years of defeat in our eyes? I suppose that would be very off putting – defeat. Like failure – everyone stays away. First rejection and then loneliness.

And please don't list ways of preoccupying myself – walks, art galleries, Canadian exercises, gardening. Amnesty one day, a sick friend the next. I do it very well, even happily, making notes to myself about interesting radio programmes and books I imagine will help me make sense of this…this…this 'seething' life. Even a tiny corner of it. And after it I'm lonely. Desperately, painfully, heart-achingly lonely. I sometimes think I'm dying from lack of love. Loved by no one, touched by no one. Not even a child. If someone, somewhere doesn't put their arms round me in *real* love one of these days I think I'm going to die.

Pause.

See what I mean? Me me me me me! We came here to face your identity crisis.

Pause.

Or was that just your excuse to get me away from my problem.

Pause.

Why is everyone unhappy?

KENNEDY deliberately breaks the mood.

KENNEDY: Funny you should ask, Miss Mathews.

GERTIE catches on.

GERTIE: Yes, Mr Phillips, why is it that everyone is unhappy?

KENNEDY: Identity crisis

He executes a music hall skip and spreads his arms.

Pah poum!

GERTIE follows with a similar jump.

GERTIE: Identity crisis, Mr Phillips?

KENNEDY: Identity crisis, Miss Matthews. We all fall in love with the wrong image of ourselves.

GERTIE: You mean *(Another little jump.)* …?

KENNEDY: I mean *(Jump.) you* fell in love with an image of Mrs Ordinary Everybody

GERTIE: And *you (Jump.)* fell in love with an image of Mr Divinely Touched Artist

277

KENNEDY: When in fact *(Jump.)* I'm Mr Mammon –

GERTIE: And I'm *(Jump.)* Mrs Actress.

> *Pause.*

> *GERTIE's gaiety deflates.*

Can we go home now?

KENNEDY: Didn't help?

> *Pause.*

GERTIE: Could you fall in love with me, Mr Phillips?

> *No response.*

Ah!

> *Pause.*

It seems to me that every decision I've ever made has been the wrong one.

KENNEDY: You mean like coming here?

GERTIE: I mean like falling in love with the wrong man at the right time and the right man at the wrong time.

> *He puts his arms around her.*

No, not like that. Not for comfort, Mr Phillips. I'm not looking for comfort.

> *She disentangles herself.*

Come. Let's go home. We've solved your problem.

KENNEDY: Not really.

GERTIE: Kennedy, please.

KENNEDY: I still deeply, desperately, passionately, yearn to be an artist.

GERTIE: Divinely touched!

KENNEDY: To illuminate the chaos.

GERTIE: Mammon. More practical. *Copes* with the chaos.

KENNEDY: My soul is elsewhere.

GERTIE: I read once that philosophers deny the existence of a soul.

KENNEDY: Fuck philosophy.

GERTIE: *(Bitterly.)* Fuck art!

KENNEDY: *(Shocked.)* Gertie!

GERTIE: *(Mocking.)* 'Gertie'.

KENNEDY: That's shocking.

GERTIE: 'That's shocking'.

KENNEDY: I didn't ever think I'd hear you say…

GERTIE: 'I didn't ever think I'd hear you say…'

> *By which time they've left the beach muttering, mumbling, mocking…*
>
> *A wind seems to be gathering.*
>
> *The sea sounds wilder.*

SCENE FIVE

GERTIE's flat. Some days later. Evening.

GERTIE and KENNEDY sit in the shadows. They have simply not bothered to put on the lights.

GERTIE: When I close my eyes I'm filled with a passionate desire to do it all again – better. Infinitely better.

KENNEDY: When I close my eyes…the sea…a mango tree at the back of the house…a sugar-cane tree further down the road…children playing…on a beach…the sun…

> *Pause.*

I should be going. Curtain comes down soon.

GERTIE: Know how I was born? One night my father *insisted*. Mum told me. She actually told me: 'Your father insisted'. I'm not the product of love but of my father's impatience.

KENNEDY: My passion is fresh bread and salmon. When I close my eyes...my grandmother carrying a basket of fresh bread on her head...salmon being sold on the beach...I hear shouting...a huge moon...the sea again...children bathing there...

GERTIE: Chekhov used to say 'Work! In work is salvation'. *(Beat.)* He wrote comedies you know!

KENNEDY: Is that how you survive, humour?

GERTIE: You've got it. Black humour.

> *Both recognise the sensitive area of language.*

You going to walk out on me?

KENNEDY: You could have said 'gallows' humour.

GERTIE: Sorry. Gallows humour.

KENNEDY: You give in too easily, Gertie. 'Black' applied to the richest vein of humour seems pretty honourable to me. In fact I believe we should take humour to extreme ends of black irony. Perhaps I should be a stand-up comic! Of black black-satire.

> *He does a short stand-up comedian act, addressing an imaginary audience.*

My black brothers I say to you, I have a dream, I *have* a dream: become white! Nose-job, skin-job, hair-job, lip-job. Whatever job can be jobbed – take it. God just made a mistake. You're really white. White man, stay out of the sun in case you get mistaken for a mistake!'

GERTIE: You're taking risks.

KENNEDY: And risks must be taken. I mean I'm not one of your blacks with a chip on every shoulder, you know, looking for offence round every corner. I'm one of your thoughtful blacks, your well-read blacks, your classical music blacks. How often have you heard me call you 'guy' or 'man'? When did you ever see me with a Walkman wrapped round my ears shuffling to a thump thump thump thump?

GERTIE: You mean g'dum g'dum g'dum g'dum?

KENNEDY: You want to know my biggest shame? I can't even dance. There! My entire body is dislocated.

GERTIE: *(Coyly.)* I can't believe that.

KENNEDY: Well you go g'dum g'dum g'dum g'dum and see what happens.

GERTIE: It's not really g'dum g'dum g'dum g'dum is it? I mean, the beat of black music is a little more complicated than that, isn't it?

KENNEDY: What do I know?

GERTIE: Let's play some.

KENNEDY: You mean you've got tapes of black music?

GERTIE: Not your advanced Kiss FM stuff, but –

> *She's sorting through her tapes.*

– some Lionel Ritchie.

> *She puts on a tape which lands in the middle of either 'Dancing on the Ceiling' or 'All Night Long'.*

There, that beat's simple enough. Try this.

> *She demonstrates a simple movement.*

> *He attempts to follow but, as he warned, he seems disjointed.*

No, no, no. Like this.

> *There follows a comic scene in which GERTIE attempts to lead him through simple steps and he fails*

miserably until – suddenly – he picks up – follows – and, incredibly, flows with her.

He's been lying. He could dance all the time but he still pretends it's the first time.

KENNEDY: Hey! I can dance! I can dance! Watch me, mother, I'm a real black man after all. I got rhythm, man, and I can dance.

At which they both go into a dynamic dance routine.

It's an exhilarating scene (requiring expert choreographing).

They're puffing.

Long pause to recover.

KENNEDY: See! The soul of an artist!

GERTIE: Give me the Hamlet speech.

KENNEDY: Now?

GERTIE: Now!

KENNEDY: It's late, Gertie. I've got to be there for curtain down.

GERTIE: Five minutes.

KENNEDY: You want to decide my future in five minutes?

GERTIE: You want to be an actor? Give me the Hamlet speech.

KENNEDY rises to perform.

Long silence before starting.

He delivers it woodenly. It's obvious he's no actor.

KENNEDY: *To be, or not to be, that is the question:*
Whether 'tis nobler in the mind to suffer
The slings and arrows of outrageous fortune,
Or to take arms against a sea of troubles,
And by opposing end them? To die, – to sleep, –
No more; and, by a sleep, to say we end

The heart-ache and the thousand natural shocks
That flesh is heir to, – 'tis a consummation
Devoutly to be wish'd. To die, – to sleep; –
To sleep! perchance to dream; – ay, there's the rub...'

> *He only manages to offer this first part before* GERTIE
> *stops him and, with surprising efficiency assumes the*
> *role of director.*

GERTIE: Start again. But listen to yourself – you're delivering
each line the same way. You're going up and then coming
down, like a line of little hills.

> *She demonstrates.*

Forget the poetry, just for now. Forget it's the immortal
Bard, just make sense of the lines. Imagine you're asking
yourself a question: 'should I live on or give up?' It's the
most important question in your life. Or, to bring it nearer
home: 'to be Mr Divinely Touched Artist or Mr Mammon?
Mrs Ordinary Everybody or Mrs Actress?' Go!

KENNEDY: *'To be, or not to be, that is the question:*
Whether 'tis nobler in the mind, to suffer
The slings and arrows of outrageous fortune,
Or to take arms against a sea of troubles,
And by opposing end them? – To die, – to sleep, –
No more...'

> *Again the little hills. At which she declares–*

GERTIE: Mammon!

> *She strides to her tape recorder to rewind the song*
> *they've just danced to.*

You're a hopeless actor. Get your image right – make
money! Don't fall in love with an artistic soul you haven't
got. Mammon! Don't be ashamed! Dance!

> *By which time we're back to Lionel Ritchie and they*
> *dance their dance routine again.*
>
> *They're both high, high, high.*

Suddenly KENNEDY looks at his watch.

KENNEDY: Gertie! Curtain down! I must fly! Do you realise you've shattered my sweetest dreams?

GERTIE: That's what sweet dreams are for, sweet man. Life is richer. Get the image right and you'll find life is richer. Trust me. Fly!

A swift kiss. Gone.

She takes up dancing where she left off.

GERTIE: Look at me, mother! Better than the Harmer girl. Always was and always will be and I'm dancing with a black man half my age. Love, lust and absolutely no guilts whatsoever which I hope is making you turn in your grave. *(Listens.)* What's that you say, what? *(Listens.)* I don't care if he doesn't love me, I don't care if he's the right man at the wrong time cos it's spring, mother, wild, wild spring. So turn! Turn, turn, turn, turn…

Lights Down.

The End.

GLOSSARY OF FINANCIAL TERMINOLOGY

Directive
Written instructions to the Federal Open Market Committee to the Federal Reserve Bank of New York, regarding the conduct of open market operations.

Charge Account
A loan facility that is renewed as it is repaid and which may, therefore, be used repeatedly.

Money supply
The quantity of money in circulation in the economy.

White knight
A company subject to an unwelcome or hostile bid may invite a second bid from a friendly company as an alternative to succumbing to a takeover. That company is a 'white knight'.

Opening price
The price at which a security is quoted when a stock exchange, or other market, opens for business in the morning.

Elastic currency
The doctrine that a domestic currency should meet the needs of trade, through a stable relationship between the expansion of business activity and the expansion of credit.

Liquidity
In general, availability of funds to meet claims.

Open mouth operations
Expression used to describe the Federal Reserve's use of public statements to induce a change in money market conditions.

Risk capital
Long term funds invested in enterprises particularly subject to risk, as in small or new ventures.

Placing
The sale of new shares to institutions or private individuals, as distinct from an introduction or offer for sale.

Overnight money
Money placed in the money market for repayment the next day.

Dividend
The amount of a company's profit which is distributed to ordinary shareholders.

Order
An instruction from a client to a broker dealer to buy or sell a security.

Tender
Generally, to offer a payment as in a written offer to purchase or to offer a service in response to advertisement.

Yield
The income from a security as a proportion of its current market price.

Complete text of *Ozymandias* by Percy Bysshe Shelley

I met a traveller from an antique land
Who said: Two vast and trunkless legs of stone
Stand in the desert. Near them, on the sand,
Half sunk, a shattered visage lies, whose frown,
And wrinkled lip, and sneer of cold command,
Tell that its sculptor well those passions read
Which yet survive, stamped on these lifeless things,
The hand that mocked them and the heart that fed:
And on the pedestal these words appear:
'My name is Ozymandias, king of kings;
Look on my works, ye Mighty, and despair!'
Nothing beside remains. Round the decay
Of that colossal wreck, boundless and bare
The lone and level sands stretch far away.

OTHER ARNOLD WESKER TITLES